# Rubber Bands on My Socks

The Reflections of a Sharecropper's Daughter -
Family, Poverty, Potential and Progress

Annie P. Wimbish, Ed.D.

outskirts
press

# Dedication

This book is about my reflections, perceptions, and recollections of family and life in the south as a youth to transitioning into adulthood. Know that my thoughts may differ from those of my siblings and others who are mentioned, but these are my thoughts. I believe that many can write their names in the text and retell shared stories.

This book is dedicated to

- my wonderfully supportive husband and friend, Ray, who has encouraged and pushed me to complete the penning of my story.
- my parents, Johnnie and Annie Mae Richardson. Though not perfect, they taught the six of their children about leadership, self-respect and love for family.
- my siblings – Johnnie, Jr., Bessie Mae, Moses (BB), Willie (Ed), and Emma (Dean) who have

laughingly always been supportive of my zest to grow and learn.

- my son Draper who was my inspiration for working hard to get out of poverty.
- my niece and nephew, Myesha and Marco, who are really my "children" and share the inspirational spot with Draper.
- my son Tavon who brought me joy, just by being a part of my life.

# Special Thanks

to Dr. Linda Gilliam, Retired Educational Administrator and my editor, who demonstrated a great deal of patience as she used her expertise to support this project.

to Brenda Roberts, my friend in Savannah who has patiently addressed many of my questions through the publication process.

# Table of Contents

# PART I.
# CHILDHOOD IN
# THE HILLS

# 1

# The Family:
# Daddy, Momma
# and the Rest of Us

The Family: Front Row (L to R) Emma, Annie, Bessie. Back Row
(L to R) Johnnie, Jr, Willie (Ed), Johnnie, Sr. (Daddy), Moses (BB).
Absent: Annie Mae (Momma)

*"You don't choose your family. They are
God's gift to you, as you are to them."*
— Desmond Tutu

**The imagination serves** up all kinds of images as a child. Hearing old folk talk of times gone by adds flavor and stirs up the imagination even more. In the 40's and 50's, midwives delivered babies on the farm, and my delivery was no different. Born to sharecroppers Johnnie and Annie Mae Richardson in Halifax County, Virginia, the midwife was busy for the Richardson family, delivering baby after baby: Johnnie Junior, Bessie Mae, Moses Thomas (BB), Willie Elvin (Ed), Emma Nadine, me, and Baby Christine. Baby Christine lived only a short time, for she was premature. The midwife delivered the news, and Sister Bessie remembered how the family mourned. Baby Christine's death was not an occurrence I remembered or understood as a child.

Our earlier years shape our lives, at least that's what research says. As I have lived, I believe research just may be right. Our families add the spice of life to our growth and development. Whether good or bad, the family with whom we live and grow help to determine, to some extent, who we are as we grow. Let me be clear. How about this: Blaming or claiming family does not decide the road we choose to travel, whether it ends in defeat or greatness. The experiences, sometimes called baggage, guide us. We learn and grow or veer off onto a bumpy road. Nonetheless, we own the baggage filled with family dynamics and experiences that shape our very fabric. For knowing from where we come helps forge our path in life--- Family, the very source of our DNA.

## THE FAMILY

### Daddy: The Rolling Stone

*Papa was a Rollin Stone* boomed from a passing car, as I sat on my front porch. The popular tune conjured up memories of my Daddy, Johnnie Richardson, for The Temptations' 1972 hit described him so aptly. Never a stranger, Daddy took center stage wherever he went, and he went everywhere in our small community. Weekends called him, and we tagged along on visits to relatives, Aunt Clare Belle, L.C. Poole, and others. It was as though the crowd waited for him, and he did not disappoint. Ever the party favorite, Daddy's entrance into any social gathering was a James Brown glide, smooth like silk; his steps crisp and orchestrated like Sammy Davis, Jr.; and his jokes likened those of Richard Pryor, quick and witty, with a timing that kept the crowd rolling in laugher, tears flowing, asking for more. Oh, Johnnie Richardson knew how to draw in a crowd. It was his calling card.

Daddy. His Man Cave

Johnnie Richardson - Dressed to impress!!

My Daddy's social life gave a glimpse of the creative visionary that was within. With no training, he often drew specs on scraps of paper, built sheds from those scraps, and repurposed old planks and tins from dilapidated buildings. He used wood cut with an axe from his own hands, a hand saw, and his vast imagination. Big farm families needed sheds back then, and my family was no different. In one makeshift structure, you'd find meat slaughtered on the farm smoked and cured. This process preserves the meat for later use. Another housed grain and wheat from the harvest season. Onions hung from the ceiling in Momma's old stockings, and sweet and white potatoes laid bare on the floor for preservation.

Daddy's additional structures included the chicken coop. Let me say that no one escapes the smells of a farm; sometimes the smells competed just to see which would win. The hogs and the chickens offered heavy competition. Don't let the chickens fool you. Maybe the coop itself contributed to the stench marinating from the chicken house at night. Built from leftover wires, string and wood planks, the coop allowed chickens to come and go at will, freely roaming the yard by day, walking in their own waste and leaving, well---a funky mess that reached our noses at night. What I know for sure is that farm work necessitated shared hands from neighbors. From this, I experienced true community spirit.

Of all the sheds built by my Daddy, the Man Shed was the most interesting. In it, Daddy made, stored and served his home brew. This alcoholic drink made from a concoction of potatoes, peaches, black berries, or whatever was in season, created a potent mixture. Daddy's friends, near and far, came and went year- round to savor this premium brew. They enjoyed evenings of heavy drinking and thumping blues, B.B. King or Aretha Franklin on the record player, or Daddy strumming his second-hand, two-string guitar. Much lying and bragging occurred in this shed. From the thin walls of the house, we heard loud laughter and handclapping. We huddled and wondered at the fun they must have been having.

The Man Shed remained a mystery to us kids. Daddy kept us at bay. It was strictly off limits. Oddly enough, however, when my sister Emma and I turned three or four, Daddy summoned us to the Shed to dance for the men, while he strummed the two-string guitar. Emma and I jumped and twirled with little girls' joyful glee. We pleased our Daddy, and he showed us off. He bragged on how smart we were and how he taught us to dance. The men threw quarters at our feet. We gathered up the quarters. Daddy ushered us out, and we left beaming and dreaming of how we would spend our bounty.

A farmer's work never ends. Providing for a family's needs on a farm means earning monetary revenue as well. A successful farmer gains a reputation by the sale of his wares. Johnnie Richardson's reputation spread throughout Halifax County into Danville City. Daddy was a prolific gardener, a gardener among gardeners. Saturday mornings found the family loading the car up with red-ripe tomatoes, round green watermelons, cantaloupes, fresh picked black-eyed peas, string beans, and other garden- fresh fruits and vegetables. We finished the load, watched Daddy roll the car down the hill, "pop the clutch," and cranked up the car. We jumped in and joyfully headed to Danville. There the produce sold quickly to "city folk," hungry for fresh produce. At the end of the sell, daddy gave Emma and me a quarter. I never knew how much the other siblings received, and I never asked. Emma and I spent our prize on orange slices and Spanish peanuts from Woolworth's Five and Dime in the city. Oh, how we enjoyed our Saturday trips to the city.

The 30-minute drive home from Danville on Highway 360 often took longer than it should. Many times, Daddy stopped to visit the car trunk as many as 5-6 times before reaching home. As a child I only observed and wondered. Getting older turned wonder into reality. Daddy sipped alcohol with every stop and every visit to the trunk.

In the earlier days, I recall the Danville trips brought laughter to our family. The trips brought out

the lighter side of Momma and Daddy. They told stories and laughed with each other and with us. As we grew older, the atmosphere darkened. Laughter stopped, and there was a strained tension that I did not understand as a child. I knew something changed. Violence moved in. Momma and Daddy argued and fought. I recall violent fights between them that required stops for our safety. I remember vividly how Daddy reached over and slapped Momma in the face, leaving bruises visible to anyone. No shrinking violent, Momma pounded Daddy on the head as he drove, causing the car to nearly swerve off the road. Arriving home meant a continued knockdown brawl, with Momma cursing and fussing and Daddy beating her with his fists like a man. He'd stomp her face. He kicked and stomped her stomach. He stomped her vagina. Momma fought back as viciously as she could. We cowered in the corner, crying. I prayed that they would stop.

The physical fights between Mom and Dad continued and intensified. On Fridays, after the long work week, Dad was ready for the weekend. He'd come home, take his bath, lather his face with Magic Shaving Cream, and shave it off with a two-edge razor blade. He finished grooming, by adding Royal Crown grease to the edges of his processed hair to hold back the loose ends. It completed the Nat King *like Papa*

Cole look. He gently patted enough <u>Old Spice</u> to seal the out- on-the-town deal. The fragrance lit up the house. This peacock show of "I'm my own man" infuriated Momma. Sometimes she sat in anger and watched this spectacle. Other times, she'd verbally and physically attack, and we'd witness another fight. We were so frightened. We stayed silent. I tried to hide in the shadows and hope he'd dress quickly and leave. The sound of the car driving up the dusty road to the main highway immediately changed the mood in the house. Laughter and joy returned and lasted for a while, for we knew Daddy would not return until late Sunday night.

Sometimes, Daddy returned unexpectedly on Saturday night to pick up something he had forgotten. Sometimes the return meant changing clothes for a special event not planned for. Whatever the reason, it was clear that my Daddy no longer found it necessary to respect his wife or children. His mistress came with him on those nights. She sat in the car, in front of the house, waiting for my Daddy. This blatant disrespect threw Momma into a frenzy. Like a crazed animal, Momma flew open the door with heavy objects in tow. She smashed headlights, shattered taillights, and broke the windshield on Daddy's car. It was gut-wrenching and scary for us all to watch our Momma.

As a young girl, it was beyond my years to understand why another woman sat in my Daddy's car at our house. As I grew into my teen years, the sight of my Daddy's mistress in his car became normal. The two openly displayed an affair to the public. She would sit under him in the car like two teenagers appearing as one under the steering wheel. We'd see them hug romantically at the local county fair. They'd hold hands and love on each other at neighboring house parties. Teenagers embarrass easily at whatever their parents do. As Emma and I grew into our teen years, our embarrassment was open and public. Our Dad's open affair encroached on our time to enjoy teen life. We wanted to enjoy the gaiety of parties; yet once we spotted our Dad and his mistress at the same party, we'd hide and duck, hoping he would not see us. We feared he would go home and beat our Mom for allowing us to attend.

Mom and Dad continued to fight openly and often. What confused me was the kindness he showed his children. He boasted about us and protected us with a watchful eye. He was clear, "You don't mess with Johnnie's children." He meant it and showed it once at a party where he, his mistress, Emma and I attended. As usual, Emma and I tried to duck and hide from him. That peek-a-boo was more difficult than it was worth. We gave up. Two hoodlums (Dad's words) started fussing. Daddy quickly told us to leave. He recognized when a fight might soon turn to shooting. We left quickly. I often reflect on Dad's motives. Was there really going to be a fight or was this his decoy to get us home? Fights happened at "juke joints." So, I'm thinking that this time, Daddy was right.

While my Dad tried to look out for us as children, the responsibility waned terrible as we grew into teenagers. His second family with his mistress required more and more of his time. Yes. My Dad had children by his mistress, and so, the second family. However, my earlier years are full of memories of a Dad who was attentive and loving. I remember an incident when I was in third or fourth grade. We were studying summarization in English. The teacher gave an assignment to select an article from a newspaper and write a single paragraph summary. I cried when I got the assignment. I cried not because of the task, but because my family had no newspapers. My neighbors had no newspapers. I didn't know anybody who had newspapers. I debated over whether to take the "F" for not doing the assignment or tell my parents and wondered what they would do. Getting an "F" was not part of my mode of operation as a child. When I got home from school, I immediately told my Momma. She fussed and cussed about such a crazy, thoughtless assignment from the teacher. My Momma didn't know where to get a newspaper. Momma told Daddy as soon as he hit the door. It was dark, and he'd worked the fields all day. He, too fussed and cussed about "these damn teachers not thinking about folks having to work and don't have no paper." By this time, I'm crying so hard, I'm breathless. Daddy gets in the car, drives up the driveway so fast that the dust even swirls in anger. Daddy returns with newspaper in tow. He obtained it from the Boss Man (landowner). He told me that I'd better get an A, and an A I got. That teacher never knew the turmoil that simple assignment caused in my house. Amid the chaos, my Daddy was my hero that night.

In my mind, I never thought Daddy stopped loving his children by my Momma, but the relationship grew further and further apart as he devoted more and more of his time to his second family. When Emma and I graduated high school, Dad never showed up. He never attempted to touch base with us. When his mistress's daughter graduated a few years later, Daddy dressed in all his finery, boasting and inviting the world to celebrate with his second family.

As a young girl, I thought I hated my Daddy for the way he treated my Momma and neglected us in our teen years. I am ashamed to say that there were times I'd wish he'd die in a car accident over the weekend so that he and Mom would not fight. I thank God that he did not allow an early death for Dad, but instead, gave him longevity so that I learned to love him again, deeply, in my older years. I sometimes think that perhaps God took Mom early, whom I loved deeply, so that I would have an opportunity to love my father the same way. If that was His intent, then it worked. In the end, not only did I learn to love and appreciate Dad again, but I even began to somewhat understand his actions. God has a funny way of getting our attention!

Things my Dad used to say that left lasting impacts on my life and leadership:

- Don't half-ass do things; if you're going to do it, do it right the first time. [Time-saving and attention to details]
- Get up early and do your work while your head is fresh; don't wait until it's hot or half the day's gone. [Being alert]
- Don't quit because you're tired; the work still has to be done and done right. [Endurance]
- Do what you say that you're gonna do; your word is your bond. If your word is nothing, you are nothing. [Honesty]
- Always do your best because you're Johnnie Richardson's child, and we always do good work. [Make an impression]

- There's always something to do, find it or look busy. [Open to new ideas]
- I'm going to call you once; don't let me have to call you a second time. [Sense of urgency.]

## Momma: Spitfire

Momma- Spitfire

I loved my Momma, as most folks do. I was her baby, and she made sure I knew it. As far back as I could remember, I was a clingy, crybaby who wailed if Momma left my sight. I hid behind the skirt of her ragged dress or sat on her lap every chance I had, and she'd hug and cuddle me very protectively. Maybe it was because I was such a tiny, frail looking little creature; skinny legs and body where bones poked from under my skin were signatures. Embedded in my tiny head were notably huge brown eyes, and I possessed what my older sister called a "little big mouth" as I always had something to say.

Yes, I loved sitting in my mother's lap and smelling her skin. There was something special about her skin that still resonates with me today. It wasn't because of any special fragrance, because as far as I knew, she never had any except perhaps some cheap dime-store perfume purchased at Woolworth's. No, it was her unique smell.

Mom had large hanging boobs, and in order to preserve her bras for weekends and special occasions, she rarely wore one during the week as she cleaned or hand washed laundry in the outdoor wash tub. Thursdays were wash days. She'd build a fire around the large, black cast iron pot, boil water and set up a separate wash and rinse tub; then she'd get going on the laundry. She'd scrub clothes on the wash board and dip them in rinse water doused with Little Boy Blue Bluing which made the clothes whiter. She'd twist them ferociously, with strained muscles to rid them of excess water and then hang them on the outdoor, homemade wired clothesline to dry in the blowing wind and hot sun. This was a full day's task that I admired as she seemed so organized. Winter, summer, spring or fall, this was the Thursday routine. During the tobacco harvesting season, this Thursday task took place after she'd worked at the barn preparing tobacco most of the day. There were days when Daddy would turn the headlights of the car on the clothesline so that Mom could see how to hang the clothes as night fell and she completed the laundry task.

Momma told stories with laughter. Her favorite past times included visiting her mother, my maternal grandma whom we called MaMa and her sisters, Aunt Mary and Aunt Elsie. She visited Aunt Mary more because she could walk there; otherwise, she would rarely be able to visit. Daddy had the only transportation, and this conveyance took him to spend the weekend with his mistress. Country walking was 2-3 miles, but with Momma holding my hand all the way, it wasn't too bad, especially as I searched the woods for monsters on our way back home at night.

I carry a sad image of my Momma. Anger enraged her, and her body caved into physical hurt. The reality is that Daddy openly cheated on her and physically beat her. It left a hardness that caused her to curse like a sailor at times, but often through a pool of tears. As she cried, I cried. She tried desperately to comfort and console me, saying, "Everything will be all right," as tears rolled down her cheeks. She wore loose, often ripped clothes that were held together with safety pins. I remember the days when Momma joyfully went with Daddy and the family to town to sell the farm's produce. She happily visited friends on the weekends because Daddy loved to socialize. That relationship ended at some point, and I don't know how or when. Momma's life regressed into visiting MaMa and aunties when not at home in the old shack.

Though I'm no medical doctor, I believe that the stress from the physical beatings that my mother endured, and the strain of a known mistress and second family contributed to her high blood pressure. She took medication but was often unable to get the needed medicine. To stretch the supply, she often took half the recommended dose. My mother suffered a stroke, which left her right side slightly paralyzed. The paralysis did not stop her from visiting MaMa and her sisters. She'd limp on that right leg down the highway with us tagging along. She wanted and needed to be with her family. They were all she had left. Besides, she knew how much Emma and I enjoyed hanging with our cousins, and we were too young to go alone. One thing for certain, my

Momma, though sad, was a true fighter, high spir-
ited, and stood up to a challenge. She held her own.
I know that this was a major indirect lesson I learned
from her.

Things my mom used to say that impacted my life
and leadership:

- Treat people right because you never know
  who you will need in life. (Responsibility)
- Even though he's sorry, he's still your Daddy and
  you will respect him. (Respect for authority)
- Don't go up to that school acting like a fool,
  or I'm coming up there and act like one too.
  [Education is important.]
- I'll beat the black off you. [Consequences and
  Accountability.]
- You're just as good as anyone else out there.
  Don't let anybody tell you nothing different.
  (Confidence & Asset thinking)
- Life is hard. Just do the best you can – always.
  [Endurance]
- Watch out for the people you hang out with;
  some of them mean you no good. [Discernment
  & Association]
- You can't do what everybody else does because
  you'll be the one to get caught. You do what is
  right. [Self-monitor.]

## Johnnie Junior: The One in Charge

Large and in charge describes my oldest sibling, Johnnie. When Momma and Daddy left the house, they left him in charge, and he never let us forget it. "I'm the boss," he'd say. "Y'all better listen to me." He loved watching The Three Stooges show, ---Larry, Moe and Curly—and often put Emma and me behind the bed and would tell us to "Shut up and be quiet," so that he could continue to watch his favorite shows. Sometimes he made us go outside and play. Johnnie Junior showed brotherly kindness at times. He would walk Emma and me up to the tobacco barn near our house where a flat-bed sat, not hitched to anything. He'd put Emma and me on the back of the trailer and he'd stand near the hitch. With our weight on the back and his strength in the front, he'd lift the hitch and pull it back to the ground as we enjoyed our see-saw ride. Emma and I screamed with glee. This happened frequently until one day the trailer end hook smashed his foot. Johnnie screamed in pain. The foot wasn't broken, but the skin was ripped. Mom doctored it up, and he hobbled around for several days; doctor visits back then were rare and reserved for serious illnesses. There was neither money nor insurance for medical bills. Johnnie's attitude of bossiness never left, even as we matured into adults. Whenever we came together as a family, he always reminded us that "I'm still the one in charge."

Though we all knew Mom loved all of us, Emma and I used to sometimes wonder if Johnnie was her favorite. When he became a young adult and moved away, she would get so excited when he came back home to visit. As we look back, we think part of the excitement may have been her knowledge that Johnnie would give her money that she used to purchase her blood pressure medicine and sometimes bought little treats for us. Hmmm.

Even though his bossiness continued into his adult years as Emma and I grew in our older years, we loved visiting him and his wife, Mary Ann. We knew that there would always be something good on the stove, and Ann would greet us with a big, unique laugh. At any rate, though Johnnie Junior spoke rough- ly and in a gruffy manner, we later realized that he was really a big teddy bear of caring.

### Bessie Mae: My Diva

I absolutely adored my oldest sister Bessie Mae. She was two years younger than Johnnie. The two would often fight (literally and figuratively) for the leadership role of being "in charge." Seven years my senior, I used to look up to Bessie Mae with eyes of reverence. She defined beauty, and I used to wonder if I would look as pretty as she when I grew up. She inherited a lot of responsibility for taking care of Emma and me. She fed us, bathed us and combed our hair as Momma worked in the field. She also prepared three home-cooked meals daily for the eight of us.

Oh, how I hated Bessie combing our nappy hair, as she graphically described. Both Emma and I had short, thin, soft hair no greater than two inches long that would knot up fiercely from wind and sweat as we played outside. Bessie would drag the comb through the short-interlocked pieces mercilessly as she fussed at us for having such "nappy" hair. She'd make what seemed like a million plaits braided so tightly that it felt like she was squeezing the skin out of our scalps. Even though we'd cry, she'd jerk our heads back saying, "We've gotta comb these naps. Keep your head still. You should be glad someone is combing this barb wire [her reference to our thin, stringy locks]."

We often asked for ponytails like our cousins who had 18" long, thick, wavy locks. She'd harshly remind us that we didn't have enough hair for pig tails, let alone ponytails. After a washing of our hair, semi-monthly, she'd use the hot comb to "straighten" out the pieces. She'd lay the iron comb on the wood stove until it was nearly red -hot, divide our little pieces of hair into small portions and drag the scorching comb through from the root to the crest. I could actually hear the comb sizzling through the hair and frying the packed Royal Crown hair dressing. So many times, I felt the heat sear the scalp. On many occasions, we walked away with tiny pig tails and scalp and ears infested with little blisters. As we cried out, Bessie would jerk our heads back and say "Sit still, and I'll stop burning you." When completed with the task, she would add some grease from fat back pork to soothe the burn. We may have been in pain, but the end result was always a beautiful look.

When I was around 11 years of age, Bessie married a military guy. She lived home for a while as her husband made living arrangements on the west coast. As is customary for military wives, she began to receive allotment checks. Through this opportunity for her, she began to expose the rest of the family to new experiences. For example, she introduced us to homemade spaghetti. Because of her, we had our first ever real Thanksgiving dinner with a baked turkey and stuffing. Before that, I thought those things only happened on television. Bessie later moved to San Diego and visited home in Virginia sporadically for the next decade. I did not get to know her well until our later years in life.

### Moses (BB):The Reserved One

My brother BB (as we called Moses) kept to himself a lot. He was quiet and managed to be so organized in a house of chaos. For example, though we had little to no private space of our own as we shared the rooms together, he always had a "secret spot" for his stuff. He'd put his Vaseline and tooth paste in a box or some type of container in an orderly fashion and hide it. Even in hiding it, he'd mark the container with a pen or pencil to indicate the resting point of content at his last use (Vaseline) so that he'd know if anyone had been in it. Dean and I would sometimes find his stash and try to sneak a little. As a general rule, we didn't have Vaseline or toothpaste in our house, and we were in awe of him with it. Not having household tooth paste and toothbrushes as a norm may have been the reason we often spent many sleepless nights crying with tooth aches and waking in the mornings with half of our face swollen, sometimes twice the normal size. We suffered teeth that had become abscessed with infection in the surrounding tissue and bone. Oh, so many painful, tearful nights!!!! Anyway, back to BB!!! I so admired his orderliness, cleanliness and strategic thinking about how to be better in a really challenging situation and how to preserve what he valued. I now wonder if he had a touch of Obsessive-Compulsive Disorder (OCD); but then again, that describes me too – wanting order and structure.

When he was a teenager, BB was burned badly, so badly that we thought he might die. He had 3<sup>rd</sup> degree burns over three-quarters of his body. I remember the incident so vividly, though I was only around nine or 10 years old. Daddy, Momma, Dean and I were at a funeral near Danville, VA. It was summertime, maybe in July. A police officer came to the church as we stood outside among the crowd talking after the funeral. The police officer stated loudly, "I'm looking for a Johnnie Richardson." Daddy, in his humorous way said, "I'm one Johnnie Richardson. Some call me J.R." The officer asked if he had a son named Moses. I could then see the fear in Dad's and Momma's eyes. The officer told us that we needed to get home right away because Moses had been burned. My parents were so puzzled and tried to ask questions, and the officer said forcefully, "You need to go now." We jumped in the car and speedily tailed the police officer home to learn that Moses had been taken to Richmond, VA to the medical center. Daddy and Momma quickly dressed to make the nearly two-hour trip to Richmond. While Mama waited in tears and the rest of us in fear, Daddy went to the landowner to ask for money to fund the trip to Richmond. I can't remember if Dad drove or a friend/relative drove them to Virginia Medical Center. I do remember that we all cried most of the night as we were all so worried. We did not know if "BB" was alive or dead. Mom eventually called back and through her tears, informed us that he was alive, but it did not look very hopeful as she described his condition.

Over time, Mom and Dad made the trip regularly and began to get positive reports from the doctor. BB's recovery was long, slow and painful as his discolored body began to regain color. Thanks be to God, Moses recovered fully. Miracles do happen!

### Willie (Ed): The Adventurer

Willie, or Ed as we called him, is the youngest of the boys and one that I often relied on as an adult. As a child, however, for some reason, he and I often literally fought in the field beside our house each day. Well, I'd try to fight him [can't remember any of the reasons why], but he was my senior by four years and several inches taller than me. With his height overshadowing me, it was easy for him to hold my forehead with the palm of his hand and keep his body out of the reach of my tiny frame as I'd tried to attack him. I would be so mad at him because I couldn't actually strike him, and he'd say, "Now go on Anna Bell; leave me alone."

Ed can be described as adventurous, mischievous, a risk-taker, always willing to try new things. He was very giving and forgiving, not holding onto grudges. His hand was always open to help. Ed taught me how to drive using his olive green, 1972 Nova. He was the one to take me to Division of Motor Vehicles in Danville, VA to get my driver's license, driving that same automobile. Ed again came to my rescue when I worked at Dan River Mills in Schoolfield, VA. We worked in the same department; he was likely responsible for me getting the job. I was a weaver, and he was a lead person. I had such a hard time keeping my looms running and would cry every night – we worked second shift, 4 – 12 pm. He would use his weaving reed and try to help me get the looms started so that the overseer would not fuss at me. Oh, how I hated that job, and how glad I was to leave. Ed was likely even happier than I was.

Ed's help and support did not stop there. As teenagers, Emma and I often hung out with Ed and his friends, enjoying yard parties, going to the drive-in theatre, and traveling to the local fair. We had fun. As I became an adult, Ed was often the loan officer when I needed financial support. I always paid him back because I knew there would likely be other times when I'd have a financial need; these needy times were quite frequent. He was a generous soul. I learned much from him, gaining many worldly exposures, some best not noted here.

### Emma (Dean): The Protector

Ok, here's Emma, at last, the one that I've referred to several times earlier. Emma and I were, and still are, like peanut butter and jelly, macaroni and cheese,

Mutt and Jeff; we were always together. Emma (most often called Dean, the name that will frequently appear simultaneous in this book) and I are 18-months apart in age and grew up in sync; it was always Dean and Anna Bell; Emma would declare that it was always reverse order - "Anna Bell and Dean". [The 'Anna Bell" is another story for another day.] Anyway, Mom dressed us alike, and Bessie Mae combed our hair the same style as children; people often asked if we were twins. In our youth, we practically lived in the woods playing in our make-believe playhouse, climbing trees, picking wild berries and plums, playing rhyming games, and yes, dancing for Daddy and his friends for quarters. Oh, such fun!

Along with brother Johnnie, Emma and I watched a lot of cowboys and Indian shows on our tiny, 10-inch black and white television. Our play replicated our viewing as we used small tree limbs for our guns and shorter sticks for knives. Being farmers, our brothers had small pocketknives. One day, Emma and I decided to use one of these small knives (maybe a 1" blade) in our "play" fight. Emma was on top with me pinned down holding off the blade. My arm grew tired, and I let go. The blade found a home in the center of my forehead and lodged itself there. (I still have the mark to prove it.) Momma spanked us both, and with each stroke of the dogwood switch that she made us gather, she explained how we could have been seriously hurt and what will happen should she catch us with a knife again. She never did!!!!

As a teenager, Emma was the aggressive one, the protector. I would run off at the mouth and get into trouble with other girls wanting to beat me up. Emma would come to my rescue, ready and willing to fight for me as I stood back and often cried. Generally, she was the quiet one until someone roused her, especially if it appeared to be a threat to me. I was so skinny, and I so admired Emma because she was brave, plump with big legs and beautifully developed boobs as we grew.

In our early adult years, Emma and I rented a house and raised our children together. You will read more about this experience and Emma's major role in my life in another chapter.

### The Other Brothers

From arguments of my parents, I grew up knowing that I had other siblings from my Dad and his mistress. I later discovered that I had four additional handsome brothers, not much younger than me, who have a striking resemblance to Dad – Grover, Marvin, John and Johnnie Wayne. At this point in my life, my knowledge about them is growing, and I pray that we may continue to become closer.

*I come from a large family, but I was not raised with a fortune. Something more was left me, and that was family values.*
- Dikembe Mutombo

# 2

# Our Home

*I used to dream about escaping my ordinary life, but my life was never ordinary. I had simply failed to notice how extraordinary it was. Likewise, I never imagined that home might be something I would miss."*
— *Ransom Riggs, Miss Peregrine's Home for Peculiar Children*

**My parents and** neighbors were all sharecroppers. Sharecroppers were tenant farmers who worked the land for a share of the profit and a place to live. In most cases, tenants were poor people who lived in shacks. We were those people. I recall living in several shacks with external and internal doors falling off the hinges, foot long or larger holes in the ceilings and floors, and rat infested. One house, I remember, was a two-story dwelling. It was where most of my childhood memories lie.

My grandparents, also sharecroppers, had previously lived in this house of reference on Mr. Roy Davis' farm. (Future references will be Mr. Roy, the identity used for him by his tenants.). Through some government assistance, my grandparents had been able to purchase a small, four-room house (kitchen, living room and two bedrooms). The bathroom was laid out in the specs but never completed with plumbing. When my grandparents moved to their new home with, oh, such pride, my parents and the six of us children moved into the house they left behind.

We returned to Mr. Roy's farm, leaving another shack in the Laurel Grove community. Likely Dad had been asked to move from Laurel Grove for standing up for his rights. At least, that's what I wish to believe. I do recall my sister, Bessie, telling me the story on one occasion of how Daddy kept up with his expenses for the year of sharecropping and presented this to the landowner. This kind of behavior was very unusual for sharecroppers. Sharecroppers, rarely, if ever, were provided documents and were expected to nod and accept the landowner's words of worth. When Dad's numbers disagreed with the landowner's, he was asked to leave for being "disrespectful." Whatever the reason, we found ourselves returning to

Mr. Roy's farm, moving into the home being vacated by my grandparents. Daddy said that Mr. Roy valued keeping his shacks full of "big" families because of low cost labor. This may have been the principle for most landowners, regarding sharecroppers. I do know that the families we were associated with all had lots of little heads that we often played with.

Like the other houses of my memory, this two-story house had large holes and cracks in the walls and floors, large enough for snakes to crawl in and out. One day I fearfully watched a huge black snake crawl through the dining room. I ran out of the room screaming until I was out of breath. Daddy said not to worry about the black snake because it only wanted to eat the rats, and we did have huge rats in the house. He went into the room to try to find the snake but had no luck and said it must have gone back out through the hole. Maybe the snakes were justified, but I was still petrified and would do a quick glance around the room each time I entered to ensure I saw no evidence of the slithering reptile. Daddy was right. Gigantic rats ran around the house at will. Because of the sizes of these monsters, Emma and I made up a song after "The Farmer in the Dell" and changed the words of "the cat chased the rats" to "the rats chased the cats."

I thought this was a relatively big house compared to past dwellings. On the bottom floor was our parents' bedroom, which also served as the family room. There was a "formal" living room, a second bedroom, a formal dining room and a kitchen. The second floor contained two bedrooms, each with its own separate entry steps to the lower level. In its heyday, the house must have been a beautiful home. In our day, because of the holes in the floor and ceiling, and lack of heat, my family basically lived in a fraction of it - our parent's bedroom, one upstairs bedroom, and the kitchen. Our parents' bedroom was the family's gathering place. I thought it was spacious with a bed, dresser, full size sofa, stuffed recliner, television, trunk under the stairs and space for side chairs, foot stools, etc. It was a great place for us to sit and hang out. The wood burning stove was located here, and fire burned continuously during the waking hours; late night was a different story when the fire died out. The cold crept in.

Most of the children, girls and boys, slept upstairs in the front bedroom. There were two full size beds, a twin bed, a chest of drawers and a dresser here. Initially, when I was under six, my oldest brother had his own sleeping area, the twin bed. Two brothers shared one full bed; two sisters shared the other full bed; and I slept with my parents downstairs. As my siblings grew older and moved away, I eventually moved upstairs, and the sleeping arrangements changed. There were two small windows and no direct heating source. This room was located directly over my parents' bedroom where the wood stove was located. The door connecting our parents' bedroom and this upstairs room was always kept open to allow some of the little heat to flow upstairs. The door to the back-upstairs room was always kept shut in order that heat might be retained in the front bedroom.

The back bedroom was basically used as a closet for storage. Because my grandparents lived in the house before us, I think maybe our Granddaddy had made hanging rods that ran from the front of the room to the back on both sides, with a large walkway in the middle for hanging clothes. Cardboard boxes scattered the room and were stacked in an array of angles. They were filled with various items (clothes, hats, household goods, and other articles) left from our Grandparents. In winter, we'd pull out our coats and put them on to enter, as we referred to "the freezer" We'd quickly search through the hanging garments or frantically comb through one of many piles of clothing on the floor or old trunks until we located items of choice. Then, we'd race out, slamming the door, as if one of those giant rats was hot on our heels.

My parents' bedroom was separated from the kitchen by the once formal dining room. From my parents' room, we had to pass through the formal dining room to access the kitchen. The formal dining room contained furniture left by my Grandparents, dining table and four chairs, buffet, and hutch. I remember racing through that dining room as a very small child, around 2-3 years of age, and peering over the tabletop, hungry for the homemade pound cake that MaMa had in its center. This memory was a thing of the past. This place we now inhabited, once highly lauded, had long lost most of its beauty. Holes in the floor allowed cold air from a frigid winter to dominate the room. We would often grab a jacket to move through this room to the kitchen. Unless Mom was preparing a meal, the kitchen had no heat as well.

The kitchen held our wood cook stove, a yellow vinyl top table designed for six chairs (though we did not have six chairs), self-standing kitchen cabinet with some missing doors, and a basin stand to hold the tin wash pan for hand washing. Dad kept a broken mirror over this basin for shaving purposes. Fire was kept in the kitchen only when Mom was cooking, during meals, and cleanup; thus, it too was frigid most of the wintertime – day or night.

Each room had an old ceiling fixture with a ceramic base and single light bulb that had no coverings; we generally had only one light bulb in the house, and this was normally housed in our parents' room, the gathering place. When traveling from room to room each night, we would screw that one bulb from the fixture and carry it with us to the kitchen to provide light. For quick runs to the kitchen, sometimes we'd grab old pieces of paper, screw them into a tight roll, light the end with a match and use that as our light source to travel from room to room or to locate items of need. It is simply a wonder and blessing that we did not burn the house down.

The second downstairs bedroom was referred to as the back room. Like the upstairs back bedroom, it was also really used for storage mainly because of a lack of heat. Clothes, furniture, and items not being used were literally thrown into the room. During the spring, we would go in and organize items. Sometimes, my oldest sister, Bessie, would even sleep there for a night or two. I think we were really scared to spend much time there because it was shut up so often. I always found myself looking around for snakes and rats.

The formal living room, my favorite, was cornered to this back room, my parents' bedroom and the upstairs back bedroom; the living room was off limits to us children except for special occasions, which mainly meant when we had special company, whatever that meant. Though it contained a wood stove left over from our Grandparents, fire was rarely built there in order to preserve wood, unless Bessie was entertaining guests. Entertaining was quite rare in winter. During winter, all connecting doors remained shut.

I thought the living room was beautiful; it was spacious and nicely decorated. I loved the royal blue twill covered sofa and chair with foot stool set. Maybe it had a special meaning as this was one of the first living room sets, out of many, that the furniture company had not repossessed. Generally, Dad would purchase new furniture during the harvesting season only to have it taken back after missing the first three payments a few months later. Countless times I witnessed my mother on her knees amidst a river of tears, beg the driver not to take her furniture as all of us children joined her, wailing loudly with the loss.

In the living room sat two lamp tables with lamps that often had missing light bulbs, a coffee table in front of the sofa, a floor stand stereo that sat majestically under the large front window with the home sewed curtain. On it sat a stack of albums that seemed to go on forever, by artists like Marvin Gaye, Eddie Kendricks, Kool and the Gang, Aretha Franklin, Johnnie Taylor, etc. In another corner hovered my Grandmother's floorstand, wind-up Victrola record player with records. Occasionally, on really nice spring days, whoever was in the household would gather in the living room, wind up that Victrola and skip around that living room laughing and singing to old tunes. I can't recall any of the musical artists, but I do remember just how much fun it was to see Mom laugh and joke.

A wood burning stove sat at the edge of the room. It mostly sat idle in winter to preserve the firewood for the main room. On special occasion like Christmas, we made a grand fire. During this special holiday, we decorated the cedar tree that Dad or my older brothers chopped from the woods near the house, dragged through the snow and placed in a huge five-gallon bucket. Mom would drag out the box of tangled lights and decorative bulbs. We'd sort through the broken pieces, find the best and hang them. Oh, such joy! As I grew old enough to date and entertain my own company, this remained my favorite place.

I thought Virginia winters were cold because inside our house, it seemed always cold, even with the centered wood-burning stove. To ward off the cold and critters and maintain the little existing heat in our home, Momma would stuff the cracks with old rags and newspapers. When the wind blew ferociously, it would often lift the edges of the shredded rug off the floor. The roof was in poor condition with major holes. Buckets and pales were placed throughout the house when it rained to catch the drippings to keep the furniture and beddings dry. That water was saved for laundry and to wash our bodies.

At times when the temperature inside and outside would drop, if a glass of water was left on the table overnight, it would freeze and be ice by morning. We children often slept in sweaters, wore socks on our feet, and used old socks on our hands like mittens as we snuggled close in bed for warmth. On winter mornings in preparation for school, we would often quickly jump out of bed blowing "smoke" as the heat from our breaths met the cold. I could hear my teeth clattering as I hugged myself and pulled on the cold clothes. At times, Momma urged us to lay our clothing on the slightly warmed stove to heat them before putting them on. We washed up in a tin basin filled with warm water sitting on the dresser, and we relieved ourselves in a gallon paint bucket or a five-gallon bucket. They were our "potty". For the brave souls, some tarried outside in the cold to use the outhouse; I chose the potty most often. Sometimes even in summer, I'd try to brave the outdoor toilet and found it difficult to watch maggots slithering across the floor. There was no indoor plumbing – toilet, bathtub, or sink.

Our drinking water source at this house was an outdoor pump about 50 yards from the house. It required pumping several times to "prime" it, and suddenly, a gush of water would spew from the faucet and fill the empty tin pale sitting at the base. It was Bessie Mae's job to get two buckets of water in the mornings and two in the evenings and place them on the stand in the kitchen. We'd then refresh ourselves throughout the day, sipping from the same tin dipper. Momma also dipped from the buckets for meal preparations. Every so often, we'd use water from the pump for our baths, but more often than not, rainwater was used. On some of the super cold days mentioned, the pump would sometimes freeze, and Daddy would somehow light a fire near the pump to thaw the frozen area. Sometimes he was successful and sometimes not. I was never sure how he did this.

Baths were a Saturday ritual. Momma would gather water from the roof leakage or captured rainwater. She'd heat it in the big pot on the wood burning stove and dump it into the old tin tub; the routine was to begin with me bathing first as I was the youngest, and each sibling followed with Momma being last. As we grew older and my siblings began to move away, the order and routine changed. I used to wonder what it must be like to sit in a real tub and dreamed of a toilet that flushed as seen on tv.

# 3

# Our Diet

*When you rise in the morning, give thanks for
the light, for your life, for your strength. Give
thanks for your food and for the joy of living.
If you see no reason to give thanks, the fault
lies in yourself.*

-Tecumseh

**Most of our** food was home grown. As mentioned earlier, Daddy was a tremendously skillful farmer who
grew beautiful vegetables – tomatoes, peas, corn,
sweet potatoes and white potatoes, string beans, etc.
He also raised hogs and chickens. After working in the
fields by day, Momma and us girls spent many hours in
the long, hot evenings of summer picking vegetables
from the garden and canning the goods. Canning was
done by putting the hot food in hot Mason jars on the

wood stove. The house became a sauna with the wood stove flaming at its highest possible level to maintain safe canning temperatures. We had no such luxuries as an electric fan. We would scramble to find a piece of sturdy, discarded cardboard or make an accordion fan from a piece of notepaper or old magazine page Momma may have gotten from the landowners. We ate well during the summer months, basically being vegetarians, as we ate whatever vegetables were in season, sometimes daily until the season ended.

Fall-winter brought hog-killing time after a major freeze set in, usually near Thanksgiving. It was really a bitter-sweet time for me because we'd give the baby pigs names like pets and watched them grow. It made us sad to know that they would be killed. On the other hand, it was exciting to know that we'd have meat in the smoke house.

Daddy and his buddies would get together as a team on hog-killing day. There was an element of excitement in the air that you could almost taste. The hogs were generally held captive in a pin. The identified hogs for slaughter would be separated from the rest and seemed to sense that something was different. They'd run to and fro, squealing loudly as the shooter aligned himself to shoot between the eyes for an instant kill; often the shooter was my Dad or Granddad. One shot and the hog dropped to the ground; my heart always dropped with the hog. This process was repeated until all identified hogs were slain. The hogs were then transported to the slaughter area where they were methodically dipped in what seemed a mountain of boiling water to remove hairs and then hung upside down for stripping the insides out. Finally, they were moved to the chopping area for packaging.

Momma, MaMa and other friends chopped, sliced and diced meats, to prepare for storage. All parts of the hog were preserved for eating, including the feet, ears, brains and hog chitterlings. Emma and I had the role of pouring water from an old Clorox jug, or sometimes an old bowl, into the string of chitterlings as the adult women flushed them of their inners. Oh, such an awful smell! I used to wonder, "Oh, how can anyone eat these things?" However, Momma had a gift of taking something that smelled so awful and turning it into a succulent dish, sometimes boiled and sometimes fried. Yes, such good eating!

The lavish eating of meat, however, lasted only a short while at our house. One day we'd have a smoke house bounty with pork (ham, shoulders, pig feet, etc.) hanging invitingly. The next day, it was gone. Dad would have whisked the food source away during the night. We suspected he either sold it or took it to his second family. Whatever the reason, we were left without much meat except for fatback. Thus, this often meant a long winter with many winter meals becoming fatback, hoe cakes and fried potatoes. Because of our chickens, eggs were plentiful. A bonus was that Uncle Buggie was responsible for Mr. Roy's (landowner's) industrialized-size chicken house; so we were never short of eggs.

Occasionally, Daddy would bring something from the store which was a wonderful treat. I used to love getting a piece of store-purchased bacon, sliced bread or canned peaches that we had to share eight ways (mom, dad and kids). I used to declare that one day, I would eat a full can of peaches, all by myself. Some days, Daddy would drop in with powdered milk and chunk cheese (my parents called it "gov'ment" cheese) and canned pork. I loved it all and used to wonder where it came from. Momma would angrily inform us that it came from Daddy's girlfriend. I was so confused. I later learned that they were products from a government food assistance program for people on Welfare. Our family was not in the program, and I deduced that Momma was likely correct in her assumption. Whatever the source, I was thankful to have the tasty, diverse foods.

# 4

# Farm Life

---

*"Farming looks mighty easy when your plow
is a pencil and you're a thousand miles from
the corn field."*
                              - Dwight D. Eisenhower

**During the spring,** summer and into the fall, we all
worked hard helping Daddy get the tobacco crop planted and harvested. The spring found my parents and
grandparents teaming for planting. In the earlier days of
my recollection, wooden pegs were the manual tool for
planting. The women walked the hilly rows ahead of the
men, dropping tobacco plants about two feet apart. The
men followed, punching the earth forcefully, making a
hole that spanned a couple of inches, gently setting the
plant into the hole, and pulling a mound of soft soil for
covering the tender, green, sticky plant. See Image 1.

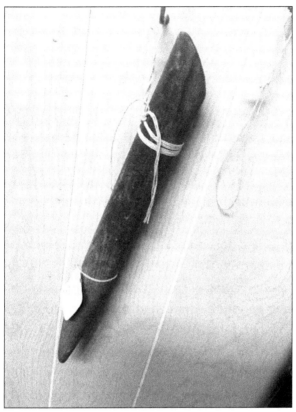

Image 1. Photo compliments of L.E. Coleman Museum

As I grew older, the peg was replaced with a hand planter that had a handle and small backing to hold water. My Momma and Dad walked side by side as if in a dance as Momma dropped the delicate plant into the planter. Dad stabbed the earth with the sharp point of the planter, pulled a trigger to release the plant and a spray of water, and lightly stumped the earth for covering of the root. Manual labor was still enforced. By the time I was in my later teens, the two-seated tractor planter was introduced to us. We thought we had arrived.

At its maturity, my brothers pulled tobacco while the girls and Momma worked at the barn preparing the tobacco for curing. Momma and Bessie strung the leaves, twisting and flipping them through twine string and securing them to tobacco sticks being held on what were called "horses". I am not sure why these were called horses because they had no resemblance to a real horse. They were basically a cross-section of planks and strips of wood connected to stand on the ground and sturdy enough to hold the six-foot stick of sewn tobacco leaves. (See Image 2) Emma, Mama and I handed the leaves in trios to Momma and Bessie. Momma and Bessie could string a stick per minute; I used to marvel at the speed that they worked. I think I may have been about six years old when I began "handing leaves", which means passing the bundle of three tobacco leaves in a fist to the stringers, Momma and Bessie.

Image 2. Cured tobacco on the "horse".
Photo compliments of L.E. Coleman Museum Halifax, VA

These were long, hot days with very little financial reward in the fall when the crop sold. Dad would sell tobacco at the warehouses. Sometimes he'd take Emma and me with him. I was simply amazed at the quick pace of the selling. The auctioneer would walk by stacked bails of tobacco neatly aligned in rows from one end to the next of the warehouse as a troupe of buyers followed him. He'd call out numbers so fast that it seemed to make my head spend. Bidders yelled their prices, and during the chaotic voices, the auctioneer would yell, "Sold" and move on to the next row. [See Image 3.] It took years for me to begin to vaguely understand what was happening. One thing I did note, however, was the fascination of how it all seemed to be in sync with the adults' level of understanding the process. As a child, I marveled at that knowledge!!!

A peek of what the warehouse floor looked like.
Image 3. *Retrieved November 11, 2018 from Google*

Leaving the warehouse led to a moment of gladness for us. Emma and I knew that it meant eating a club sandwich at a local hangout on Craighead Street or buying some Spanish peanuts and orange slices from Woolworth's Five and Dime in Danville, VA. This was the time that Daddy would occasionally purchase food from the store – that can of peaches, a loaf of white bread, Smithfield bacon. Ummm!!! I thought it was wonderful!

This life was short lived, however. There was little money. Landowners often claimed that the crop sold poorly. Daddy and other tenants had to take the landowner's word without question or be told to pack up and leave the farm immediately, sometimes overnight. No records were ever kept or presented of the sharecroppers' earnings. I often heard Daddy and other male tenants discussing the lack of fairness and how their hands were tied because they had families to feed and had to have a place to live.

We spent many days without electricity for failure to pay the electric bill. During these times, we'd use rolled up paper to travel from room to room at night (as mentioned earlier) and kerosene lamps like families from the "Little House on the Prairie." Often, I'd chuckle to myself when people asked, "Where were you when Dr. Martin Luther King, Jr., civil rights activist, was killed. I didn't know he was dead until a few weeks after his death because we had no electricity, thus, no tv. The same thing applied to President John F. Kennedy and Elvis. It seemed that seasons were not discriminating in finding us in the dark, literally.

Though poor, we had lots of fun growing up. When not working in the tobacco field, Emma and I spent hours in our "playhouse," which was usually some stacked rocks, tin cans, jar lids, old clothes Mom gave us, and sprigs placed on a bed of moss. We let our imaginations run wild as we "decorated our houses" and "baked" dirt pies and cakes, jumped rope and played hopscotch.

During the summer days in our free time, we also spent much time discovering and picking wild black berries, plums and cherries. We found large apple and pear trees that bore great fruit that someone who previously lived in the old home must have planted. We'd climb trees, sit on the gigantic limbs for hours eating our fill of fresh fruit. We'd then collect a bundle and take them home for later. In the fall, black walnuts were plentiful. We'd collect these and use a rock to smash the hard shell, pick the goodie with a needle and gobble the fine taste of the nut. One of my fondest childhood memories is Momma pulling out the old black cast iron skillet, popping field corn, and all of us gathering around the old wood heater and telling stories. Such fun!

# 5

# The Holidays

*"Holidays are all different depending on the company and time of your life."*
- Dominic Monaghan

**Thanksgiving holiday at** our home was not celebrated with a big family dinner as seen on tv. It was usually just another day with Mom scrambling to determine what she'd cook, as by this time of the year, most of the meat products from hog-killing time had disappeared from the smokehouse. A hog shoulder might have been available, and Momma would save that for Christmas. My only experience with a turkey was through tv, except when my sister Bessie married the marine. Again, there were plenty of canned vegetables from the summer gardens.

Momma took the Christmas holiday seriously. It

was baking season, and my Momma was at her best. I couldn't wait for Christmas. She'd make coconut cakes and pies, grating real coconuts. Chocolate cakes and pound cakes made from scratch were scrumptious, and among my favorites. Emma and I would compete for who would get to lick the spoon after Momma was finished with her batter.

Getting our individual Christmas bags of goodies was something we all looked forward to as well. The lunch size brown paper bags with our names written on the front generally contained one apple, one orange, a couple of whole walnuts, pecans and brazil nuts, and a sprinkle of hard candy. When funds allowed, Mom would add one or two chocolate cream drops to the bag. What a wonderful treat as this was one of those rare times we'd get fresh fruit and nuts in winter and candy like this. These wonderful treasures were savored, making them last as long as we could.

In my earlier years, I recall Daddy and Momma trying to make Christmas special for us. On this rare Christmas Eve leading into Christmas morning, a fire would be built in the living room. Daddy and Momma would play Santa and place gifts that they'd struggled to get for us under the tree. Daddy would eat the cookie we left for "Santa", and Mom would drop some crumbs outside the external door in the snow and pretend that Santa must have dropped it. We'd get so excited.

The one Christmas that really jumps out as my favorite was the year that Emma and I got Barbie dolls. Mine was a tall, beautiful blonde in a sky-blue carry case, and Emma's was a brunette in a black case. Ed and BB got pellet rifles. I can't remember what Bessie Mae and Johnny got as they were teenagers with different interest from me. Sadly, Christmas celebrations at our house became less enjoyable as Daddy seemed to be home less and less and the fighting with Momma increased more and more.

Christmas Day was always spent at our maternal grandparents' home. Momma, her two sisters (Aunt Mary and Aunty Elsie) and about 22 grandchildren gathered together there. I can remember my uncles being present, but sadly, I cannot recall my daddy ever joining us. Anyway, they'd cook a big dinner with ham, fried chicken, potato salad, string beans, cabbage, macaroni and cheese, candied yams, and the list seemed to be endless. Desserts galore, cakes and pies, graced the table. That's the one day a year that we ate to our hearts' content. Oh my!

To add to the wonderful meal that I'd dream about all year long, we children had such fun running and playing outside, all bundled up in our coats and hats; gloves were not a norm. We'd play Hide-&-Seek, Simon Says and other games as we chased each other around the house, raced, laughed and screamed until we could come in for dinner. After enjoying the mouth-watering meal, we immediately went back outside to run and holler some more. I think that my best friend and cousin, Elsie Marie, and I found everything to be funny; Emma and cousin Lorine found the same.

Our grandparents gave all of us a gift, initially. I remember getting little inexpensive dolls or tea sets that I thought were beautiful. They likely came from the Woolworth's Five and Dime store. Later, as finances became tighter, I remember the tradition becoming the teenagers received gifts and the remainder of us younger children received the infamous "goodie bag"– brown lunch paper bag containing fruit, nuts and candy. MaMa said that because of limited funding, we children would grow into receiving gifts from her and Granddaddy as we became teenagers, and this would give us something to look forward to. We younger children were so thrilled with the "goodie bag" that we didn't care.

One special gift that I remember MaMa gave Bessie Mae, and her two cousins near the same age, were white chiffon dresses with large black polka dots. Oh, I thought the teens looked like princesses, and I could hardly wait to become a teenager so that I could get something special like that. What a wonderful year! Unfortunately, by the time I reached the teenage years, the routine of gift giving had ended. I am not sure exactly why, maybe financial, health issues or both. At any rate, I never reached the "special gift" stage.

# 6

# Mountain Grove Missionary Baptist Church: Becoming a Member

*Many believe it is possible to be a "good Christian" without joining (or even attending) a local church, but God would strongly disagree.*

-Rick Warren

**At an early** age, around seven or eight, Momma announced that it was time for Emma and me to join Mountain Grove Missionary Baptist Church. This meant that when we attended the annual, five-night revival, we would go to the mourner's bench when the preacher "opened the doors of the church." Going to the mourner's bench meant walking to the front of the church and sitting on the front pew at a designated time. I am not sure why it was called a mourner's bench. I do know that I was scared and felt like crying. However, I had my sister Emma and two cousins, Elsie Marie and Lorine, right beside me; and that made it less scary. On the last day of revival (a Friday), the preacher and others gathered around us, prayed, sang, shook our hands, hugged us, some cried and shouted "Hallelujah" and "Praise God" for what appeared to be a long time (Remember I was seven or eight years old.) On the following Sunday during morning worship, we were presented to the church and were able to take part in our first Communion, drinking of the wine and eating the bread to represent Jesus' death and resurrection. I did not understand the significance of the experience at that time. Blessedly, I am totally committed now.

Momma and Daddy took us to church occasionally. It was Mr. Tot (Wallace Howerton), our neighbor, who took us to Sunday School, and later, we were transported by Uncle Lacy, father of Elsie Marie and Lorine. The seed for my understanding of what it meant to have a relationship with Christ began at Mountain Grove Missionary Baptist Church. I fell in love with Sunday School and speaking at the quarterly "MASS" meetings that occurred each fifth Sunday, as there was no scheduled worship service on fifth Sundays at most of the rural churches. Mountain Grove, New Arbor, White Oak and New Vernon, all Baptist churches, would join their Sunday School meetings and have joint studies; perhaps there were a couple of others that I don't recall. A part of this service included a friendly competition of two youth speakers from each church quoting five verses of scripture. Assigned judges would monitor the presentations, following word for word with points lost for any conflicts with verbal versus written text. Monetary awards would be presented at the end of the competition to first, second and third place winners. From this experience, coupled with becoming knowledgeable about the Word, I learned about public speaking and having confidence. I am proud to say that when participating, I was often a first-place winner. Though my mom rarely, if ever, attended the programs, she demonstrated such pride when I'd return home with my cash bounty.

As we grew as tweens and then teenagers, Emma and I took part in the many holiday programs and joined the junior choir. I later became one of the first junior ushers at Mountain Grove, one of many active roles as a youth. One of the most honored roles I was blessed to hold was being asked by the Deacon Board to follow Mrs. Mary Edmonds as the secretary of the church upon her retirement. This was quite an honor as I was a young adult in my twenties, and Mrs. Mary had been secretary for at least three decades. Talk about a humbling experience!!!!

# PART 2.
# FORMAL K-12 EDUCATION

# 7

# The Early Years

"[Kids] don't remember what you try to teach
them. They remember what you are."
— Jim Henson, *It's Not Easy Being
Green: And Other Things to Consider*

## Mountain Grove School

**I came into** the world in 1955, a year after the infamous Brown vs. Board of Education decision, a law declaring segregated schools unconstitutional and mandating schools to integrate. Historical information indicates that Virginia was in no rush to meet this mandate. It was evident in my life's journey. I attended a one-room schoolhouse my first year of school, and so did my siblings. I shall never forget Mountain Grove (See image). If I remember correctly, it served

grades 1-7, and like most southern county
it was 100% segregated. Most mornings, the
borhood children joined each other at differen, points
along the highway, depending on their alignment
in the route, and we all walked to school together-
--The Richardsons, Howertons, Glasses, Davises and
Ewells. Regardless of the weather---rain, shine, snow
or sleet, hot or cold. –we'd tread the mile or so to
school. Occasionally, Daddy would drop us off. We
often arrived before our teacher, Ms. Sarah Overby.
We called her Ms. Sarah.

**Mountain Grove**

*MOUNTAIN GROVE – This building, the newest one room school
in the county, was constructed in 1939. It is new enough for a little
repair and painting to put it in the first class condition. The ceiling
is plenty high. The large windows do not furnish quite enough light
(1/6.2). The floor space (20.2 sq.ft.) and cubic volume (242.4cu.
ft.) are ample due to the small enrollment of 36. The desks are of
a variety of sizes to provide for children of various ages. The building has no electricity.*

*There is adequate play space for the enrollment, but there is no place for a ball diamond. One of the toilets is in fair condition and one is in poor condition. The building is beside a good asphalt road. There is no evidence of a nearby water supply, and no home within an eighth of a mile.*
[Descriptor and photo taken from the archives of Halifax County Public Schools, 1988.]

Ms. Sarah lived in Danville, Virginia, about 30 miles away. We'd play outside or huddle for warmth on cold, rainy days until Ms. Sarah arrived because there was no shelter or porch on the school building. At some point, a car would stop on the side of Highway 662, in front of the school, and Ms. Sarah would exit the front passenger seat. My brothers, or one of the bigger boys, would run to the car and relieve her of her oversized, brown paper handbag full of her teaching stuff. As they held onto her large arms to support her, they would carry the bag up the small, slightly inclined red-dirt driveway to the building about 100 yards away. As she waddled up the narrow driveway, she'd engage the boys in light conversation. They welcomed the chit chat with hopes that she might give them a dime or piece of candy (which she was so good at doing) for their efforts.

Ms. Sarah was a big woman, overweight. Droopy skin covered her big arms that flapped like chicken wings when she clapped her hands. She wore floor length skirts that only revealed swollen ankles stuffed

in what we call black hospital shoes. She wou
fle her heavy body up the four to five steps, unl
door, and begin our routine for the day.

The schoolhouse opened to a large space, with a pot-bellied, coal burning stove in the center. An array of mismatched wooden benches and desks surrounded it. Parked near the front of the room was a teacher's desk where Ms. Sarah sat, and she sat a lot. I can't remember her ever moving around in the classroom for instruction. Large ceiling-to-floor windows covered the front wall of the building. They provided light. I think I recall there being only a single uncovered light fixture hanging from the ceiling. The weather outside often dictated the light inside. A black slate board covered the back wall, and there was a small storage room located behind Ms. Sarah's desk. She'd sometimes disappear there and magically reappear with chalk, occasionally construction paper and glue for art projects.

In the wintertime, some of the 6$^{th}$ and 7$^{th}$ grade boys would gather coal from the mountain of coal stacked behind the school building to build a fire in the single, pot-bellied stove. Other boys took the tin water bucket from the bench behind the classroom and carried it to the spring for the day's supply of drinking water. The spring was located deep in the woods. Sometimes Ms. Sarah would allow me to go to the spring with my brothers. I thought this was such a fun treat!!! As we waited for the building to heat and the water to arrive, the rest of us either played outside, if the weather permitted, or played inside games like jack rock and marbles, until Ms. Sarah called us to order.

We opened each day with The Lord's Prayer and the Pledge of Allegiance. Then the learning began in the open space. Each grade level sat together in an assigned area of the room in sequential order – first grade, second grade, third grade, and so on. Some students sat in scratched wooden desks decorated with carved names and love notes written inside of hearts from previous users like "Johnnie loves Judy." Others sat on long wooden benches, smoothed by years of backsides meeting wood. There was an attached perch on the back of the bench to serve as a writing platform for students who sat behind.

Ms. Sarah would call each grade level to her desk. As she sat, students would stand, and each person took a turn reading a designated passage in the order in which they stood until Ms. Sarah determined they'd read enough. She then halted their turn, highlighted the stopping point with a flare of her big arms and a ferocious attack of her red pencil. It was the signal for the next person to begin. Often the trigger for the stopping point was a misread word that she vigorously circled with that blazing pencil, and a demand followed for the reader to practice the missed word at home and come prepared to begin at that point the next day. I don't remember having any discussions about what we read; it was mostly pronunciation and maybe a few recall questions. This process was repeated until all students in that grade had a chance to read. Homework would be to practice reading the next pages; I don't know how we knew where to end "practicing" for homework. I do remember going home and reading to my mom, when we had books.

After all grade levels had participated in reading, math instruction began with the same routine. The teacher would call each grade to her desk and check problems they had been assigned to solve independently as she provided direct instruction with the reading groups. She'd again whip out the grand old red pencil, circling wrong answers. If enough of our answers met the passing standard, we'd be assigned the next lesson in the book. If not, we had to repeat with additional problems assigned. Sometimes we would get a chance to solve problems on the black chalk board using white chalk; I loved writing on the chalk board.

When we were not receiving direct instruction from Ms. Sarah at her desk, we worked independently and sometimes with the older students helping us. The only content I recall is reading and math – no other content areas like science and social studies. The closest thing to performing arts, I recall, was preparing for special programs like Christmas with each of us given parts of plays about the birth of Jesus. Easter was popular, too. We memorized assigned poems for recitation and learned new songs associated with the occasion. We'd have rehearsals, and at the designated time, perform in class with parents as the invited audience.

At the end of each school year, anxiety permeated as to whether you passed the grade or failed. All of us children knew that though we gathered around Ms. Sarah's desk by grade levels, if you were good in math and/or reading, she would move you to the next grade level. Basically, each of us could move at our own pace or learning levels. If the teacher believed you were skilled enough, at the end of the school year, she could promote you two grades within one year. This happened rarely; when it did, we students believed it was due more to favoritism than skills. Ms. Sarah also had the power to retain you, with no questions asked. We saw this happen often, especially to students she did not like very much. Of course, this opinion was through the eyes of a primary grade school child.

During recess, we played creatively outside on our makeshift playground. It was the field next door to the school, and the trees surrounded it. The boys played baseball using rocks and tree limbs as bases. We made seesaws from fallen trees or enjoyed swings made from rope hanging from a large tree with plank seats. Tag, hide-&-seek, and sometimes dodge ball, dominated the play of us smaller children. The big boys, of course, would not let us join them in their ball game.

Lunch time found us gathering outside, sitting on tree stumps, fallen tree limbs, or large rocks on warm days. We clustered together inside the building if the weather decided not to be kind. There was no cafeteria. We'd all pull out our greasy brown paper bags of goodies. My siblings and I often had a fried egg on a homemade biscuit. Our cousins usually had Treet, a canned meat product like Spam, marketed by Armour Star in the USA, and peanut butter crackers. Oh, I thought they had the best lunches. Like children do, we'd trade among the group to gain variety.

I thought Ms. Sarah was a good teacher. She would laugh haughtily and clap her hands with her huge arms waving. She knew all of us and our families by names. My mother sometimes cleaned her house on Halbrook Street in Danville, and she would give Momma sweet treats and hand-me-down clothes for us.

There were few discipline problems in our school. Maybe this was due to the connections Ms. Sarah had with the families, or maybe it was because the teacher was upheld with deep respect, next to godliness. Another possibility, however, might have been that students who attended school regularly were there by choice. Back then, dropping out of school was encouraged to support the farming needs, especially students who were challenged academically or behaviorally.

Whatever the reason, discipline issues were minimal. If any of us acted out, Ms. Sarah would beat us with a switch or paddle, tell our parents the next time she saw them, and we would get a second whipping when we arrived home. I never got a whipping from Ms. Sarah because I was too scared to misbehave, but I did see my brothers and some others get it from time to time.

Though we believed our teacher cared about us, we all knew that Ms. Sarah had her pets – two pretty girls who wore ribbons in their hair, frilly socks and pretty dresses. Unlike the rest of us students who were children of sharecroppers, these girls had parents who worked at the local factory. We thought they had much better food and clothing than the rest of us. They would bring Ms. Sarah treats, and she openly provided treats for them. For example, she would bring the two girls brown paper lunch bags of candy and proudly give it to them in front of the rest of us students. As she pulled those two girls next to her side, she'd toss a handful of candy on the floor, and watch the rest of us scramble, step on, knock, push and shove each other to get the sweet pleasures, as if we were dogs, fighting for the last piece of bread. The faster and stronger children, usually the larger boys, were the winners of the thrown candy. I would cry because I was so tiny and never able to get any. My older sister Bessie would say, "That's alright Anna Bell. We didn't want it anyway." The truth was that we all wanted it very badly.

## Mountain Road #1

Mountain Grove School closed at the end of my first-grade year, and students were assigned to Mountain Road #1, a four-room schoolhouse. Many operational processes and procedures at Mountain Road #1 were like Mountain Grove School. It was just a larger school. We still had a wood stove, outdoor toilets, no cafeteria, black slate boards and the field beside the school as our playground. However, we did become paired grade levels in separate rooms instead of one large area for all grades 1-7. If I recall correctly, the grade configuration was 1-2, 3-4, 5-6, and grade seven stood alone. This allowed us the opportunity for several different teachers during the progressive grade movement and more individual class space, as the school population increased. [See Image 4.]

Image 4. Mountain Road #1

Another difference is that there was a small convenient store about a tenth of a mile from the school. The teachers would allow the 6th and 7th grade boys to walk to the store and purchase items. The boys would go from room to room, make a list of student and teacher orders, collect money for the orders, walk to the store, and return with the goodies. BB Bats, taffy, Black Cow suckers, Mint Juleps and Banana Splits were some of my favorite candies. Most of the time, my siblings and I had little money, but friends often shared. I used to wonder, and was so impressed, with how those boys kept up with all the orders. As I reflect, it was a powerful learning experience. It taught responsibility and accountability - taking and organizing orders, keeping account of the money for each student and adult, walking safely to the store on a main highway – powerful hands-on learning.

I recall that one of my teachers in the primary grades had a sleeping disorder (I believe that it was narcolepsy). She would fall asleep in the middle of teaching. Aware that she had a disorder, she would inform me of her plans for the lesson at hand, and when she dropped off for the nap, I'd lead instruction until she bounced back.

Instructionally, we had knowledgeable, caring teachers. They insisted that we know the content. Yes, they taught content, but they also taught the importance of being kind and respectful, supportive of each other and sharing. They taught responsibility and accountability. They taught us the importance of personal hygiene and public speaking. Residual learning included the value of community and school partnerships and the need for belief and reliance on a higher power.

## Sinai Elementary School

Mountain Road #1 closed at the end of my fifth grade year, and we were assigned to Sinai Elementary School, a K-7 facility. My goodness, I thought we had arrived! We now had indoor bathrooms, a cafeteria and an official playground with equipment like metal swings, slides, and see-saws. There were many more students and different teachers – Mr. Gatha Richardson, Mr. Allen Roy Edmonds, Ms. Pattie Claiborne, and so many others. This was the mid-60s, and all teachers and students were African Americans; schools were still segregated in Halifax County. I loved the school, the new people, and the activities where teachers went outside with the class during recess. Sometimes they organized games for our fun and learning. We also began to have more extensive performing arts programs with handmade costumes that actually fit the roles. If memory serves me correctly, we had a traveling music teacher who might have come to our school to serve students once a month; the same might have applied to art and physical education.

Annie - Grade 6

At the end of 7<sup>th</sup> grade, there was an official graduation. Girls had to wear white dresses, and boys were required to wear white shirts and dark pants – very formal. My mother took on extra domestic work, scrubbing floors and cleaning houses, to earn money to purchase my white dress. Ms. Sarah, former one-room teacher from Mountain Grove School, bought me a pair of black patent leather shoes with a tiny heel; I felt so beautiful!

We were required to wear panty hose at that time, and there wasn't enough money for such in my household. On the day of graduation, Momma, who weighed in around 150 pounds, took her last pair of hose and put them on me (weighing in around 70 pounds). She tied the band of the pantyhose under my arm in a knot, and said to me, "Baby, just walk across that stage with your head held high because you are beautiful; I'm so proud of you. You are just as good as anybody else up there. You're smart, and you're special, and you're gonna be somebody one day." I remember proudly walking across the stage with my peers, in my baggy hose, singing "Climb every mountain, ford every stream, follow every rainbow until you find your dream." Yes, I felt special as I prepared to move to the big school – junior high.

# 8

# Secondary School

*"Education is the kindling of a flame, not the filling of a vessel."*

— Socrates

## Junior High School

Retrieved from Google, September 16, 2019.

**I began my** first year in secondary school as an eighth grader at Mary M. Bethune High School in Halifax County, in 1968. The grade level configuration was grades 8-12. I remember it was an all-black high school. There were a few things that really stuck out for me. Like most students transitioning to a bigger school, I was scared that I'd get lost, that people would pick on me and maybe I couldn't do the work. My Momma reminded me that I was "smart' and "special," and I believed her. The curriculum was pretty common, and I continued to do well academically. Teachers were friendly, knowledgeable and organized. Topping my favorites, however, were the opportunity for hot lunches, the quality of the food, and my eligibility for free lunch. I am not sure how we learned about free lunch; likely the school sent paperwork home to Momma, and she filled it out. I would watch the clock anxiously waiting for lunch. The homemade rolls were scrumptious; the fried chicken and vegetables were amazing. Lunch was certainly one of my favorite subjects.

For the first time, in addition to the usual subjects— math, English, science and social studies, we had electives each quarter. I absolutely loved these. Girls were ushered into home economics, and boys were directed to shop. Chorus, fine arts and other subjects were offered – so pleasing!

Because we were sharecroppers, we missed school often in the fall of the year because Daddy was responsible for completing the harvesting of the tobacco crop before the frost hit. On so many days, I cried because we could not go to school. There were times when it was even questionable whether we would attend opening day. Our misses sometimes equaled 2-3 days a week. This was excruciatingly painful as we watched the landowner's white children board the bus everyday heading off to learn. I questioned my Momma why they could attend, and we couldn't. Her response was, "That's just the way it is baby; that's just the way it is." I simply did not understand.

Being absent did not seem to affect our grades and learning as much when we were in elementary school, but missing school took on a totally different level at secondary school. We had to buy books we could not afford, and It brought much anguish for students and their families, and even for the school. Some teachers were understanding about our predicament and tried to help us by letting us use books during recess to do required homework and make up work missed. Sadly, other teachers said harsh things to us in front of the class. I think they thought that if they embarrassed us enough, we'd come to school more. I continued to be puzzled as to why teachers did not understand that we had no choice. I was often mad at my Daddy, too, because I could not understand why he'd pull us out of school. In later years, I came to learn that it was survival for him and our family. If he failed to get the crops in before the frost, we would have to immediately move off the land.

I recall one agonizingly, heartbreaking experience in my eighth-grade math class. My teacher angrily said to me, "Annie, I'm going to give you an 'F' because you need to be in school. You've missed too many days to pass." I had good grades in her class, even with being absent. I was floored. Through hysterical tears, I tried to tell her that I couldn't help being out and how much I wanted to be in school. My tears and explanation had no affect; I got an "F" that grading period, one of few, if anymore. My Momma encouraged me not to worry about the failing grade and to just do the best that I could. She reminded me that I was smart enough to make it up later. The irony was that, at the end of the semester, I had one of the highest, if not the highest, Grade Point Average (GPA) in eighth grade math that year, and I was selected by this same teacher to represent the school at a regional math competition. The teacher credited her "toughness" that propelled me to the academic status; I disagreed. What I perceived was her lack of concern, and little effort to learn about my situation. It left a hole in my heart that still burns today.

We missed a lot of schooling, and as shared earlier, often had no books. In those days, parents had to purchase books. Sometimes used books were available, but even used ones were too costly for many sharecroppers. With six children, Daddy just couldn't afford to buy them. On the few fall days when we did go to school, I'd borrow classmates' books and use every minute I could, trying to catch up on school and homework. Sometimes, I was lucky enough to have someone riding my bus, for the hour-long ride, with the same book used in my class. That was a real win.

In mid-1969, I believe, schools in Halifax County integrated. The predominantly black school, Mary M. Bethune, became Halifax County Junior High, serving the entire Halifax County school population, grades 6-8 - blacks and whites, affluent, middle class and poor. Halifax County High, the original predominantly white school, contained grades 9-12. This transition happened at the end of the first semester. When we returned to school after Christmas as an integrated group, several bathrooms and water fountains were closed and under construction with new installations. The results were new bathrooms and new fountains. I wondered why the repairs had not taken place earlier in our school life. I know there had been complaints.

Our total student body was separated in all subjects, academically, by a tracking system. We were assigned to classes according to whether our overall achievement was above average, normal, or below average, based on a standardized test. We attended classes only with students whose overall academic achievement was the same as our own, so we were told.

I guess I must have tested well each year because I was always one of the few black children in classes with white students. Two other beautiful black girls stand out. One was the daughter of a teacher on staff. Both the student and her mother were extremely fair skinned and could have easily passed for white. They had long, flowing black hair and Caucasian features. The other was a cinnamon complexion young girl with long dark hair and slanted eyes - beautiful. Both girls were well dressed, spoke articulately and always had school supplies and materials a plenty. I thought that they were both so smart. I was envious of their speech; their clothes; the materials they had to work with and loved being assigned to their teams because they were friendly and made me feel welcomed. The white kids were kind as well and accepting of me.

Because I did not have the physical beauty (I then thought), few supplies and materials, and had no real networks as they had, I was always pleasantly surprised that they invited me into their world. All my classmates seemed to know things that I did not know, and I would fake my knowledge with the right nods and smiles until I could learn what was needed to make a contribution. When we were assigned projects, I was glad to be in their groups because they had materials, and I had good penmanship. This made for a productive team (Computers were not a part of our world.).

I enjoyed most of my classes. We did things such as actively learning to write fluently, conducting research, analyzing and compiling our results. We teamed for projects, jig-sawed the learning, shared in teams, role-played the learning, participated in plays, and made presentations. I thought all classes in the school were like this until I shared my experiences with my black friends and relatives who were in the Basic and General classes. Based on their descriptions, it seems that their experiences included lecture, reading assignments and answering questions at the end of the chapters. I wondered why our classes operated so differently.

Journalism was one of my favorite classes in high school. I loved to write. I worked on the yearbook staff with Mr. Fitz, my journalism teacher. What a lovely man – round physique, bleached white hair, soft-spoken, quick smile, and big heart. As we were working on the layout for the senior pages of my senior yearbook, Mr. Fitz asked, "Annie, where's your photo?" I explained that I did not take senior pictures because we couldn't afford them. He said, "Well, we have to work something out. We have to get you in your yearbook for your senior year!" He had someone take a photo of me sitting on a hill on the school grounds, gazing in a reflective manner. This shot was placed in a prominent place in the yearbook. Oh, how special that made me feel, what affirmation!

My English Literature classes were close seconds on the favorite scale. We read books like *The Great Gatsby* by F. Scott Fitzgerald, *To Kill a Mockingbird* by Harper Lee, *Where the Red Fern Grows* by Wilson Rawls and Mark Twain's *The Adventures of Huckleberry Finn*. To this day, I still look for foreshadowing, symbolism and the like. Oh, how I loved it!!!

Physical Education ranked as my number three favorite. We were introduced to the art of golfing, gymnastics, archery, basketball. Oh, such fun! However, I hated going to the locker room to put on those blue uniforms that we called gym suits. My displeasure had little to do with the gym suits and more to do with my dingy panties and bras that were often held together with safety pins, and my baggy socks held in place with rubber bands because the elastic had long lost its elasticity. Though Momma hand scrubbed these garments on the washboard and added bluing and bleach, after many washes, over time, they simply lost their whiteness. The other girls seemed to all have pretty, frilly stuff. Sometimes, the girls would point and make fun of my ragged underwear. Trying to be the first to claim a corner in the locker room to hide and dress quickly became the norm for me.

My sister, Emma, and I graduated high school together in 1973. Our cousin Gloria, who was more like a sister to us, was the only family member attending, so she drove us in her orange Volkswagen Beetle. Our Dad did not attend; I am not sure where he was. Our mother was deceased.

# 9

# Tragic Moment

*"A mom's hug lasts long after she let's go."*
-Author unknown

**January 1973 was** my senior year of high school, and New Year 1973 entered with what I thought was harsh weather and a greater harshness in my personal world. Due to inclement weather, school was closed for several snow days. As was often the case, I dreaded snow days. It meant staying home in a cold house, and we'd miss the hot free lunch at school. Mom would certainly have us a hot meal, even if only fried potatoes and a hoe cake, but I missed the meat, vegetables, yeast rolls and dessert they provided at school.

In the early morning of January 11, 1973, we began our regular routine for the day. Momma was sitting in the black vinyl recliner, with white stuffing falling through the broken seams and leaning to one side on a broken leg. Emma and I were in this room with Momma, dressing around the wood-burning stove. BB was in the kitchen, and I am not sure of Ed's whereabouts. Bessie Mae and Johnnie lived elsewhere. My "adopted" sister (T-Bone) and niece (Karen), around ages 3-5, played upstairs in the bed, perhaps to avoid the cold. Momma called for the two youngsters to come downstairs to dress. They continued to giggle and play upstairs. At the top of her voice, she again screamed, "I said, y'all come down here right now." Suddenly, a funny, twisted, bug-eyed look came over her face, and she clutched her chest. She wheezed heavily to catch her breath. I stared at her in confusion and said, "Ma, are you ok? Ma? Ma?" Momma continued to wheeze, louder and louder. Emma and I started screaming for others. Quickly, we all gathered around calling her name, with no idea what to do. After some time, there was a final whistle-like sound. Her chest heaved, and then, stillness.

Our home was off the highway about a half mile down a muddy road that was deeply snowed in. The nearest Emergency Medical Service (EMS) was nearly 30-minutes away in Halifax. Dad wasn't home, but we all knew where he was. Our brothers, BB and Ed generally left their cars at the top of the road, about a half mile from the house, in the dirt parking area of an old, closed country convenient store, near the entry to our home. Again, I cannot remember where Ed was, but BB dashed out of the house, ran the half mile distance to his nearly snowed-in car, and drove to Daddy's mistress's house about five miles away to tell him about Mom. When Dad arrived, Mom had long stopped moving. EMS arrived a couple of hours later, loaded her up and took her away as we all solemnly looked on, feeling empty. She was officially pronounced dead at the age of 44. She would have turned 45 on her April 19th birthday, had she lived.

I loved my Mom and felt like my world was shattered because I was her baby. She always told me how smart and special I was and how I was going to be the one to make it and "be somebody one day". Before her death, after school each day, she would ask me about my work and what I'd learned. I often tried to climb onto her lap, even as a teenager, but she'd gen- tly push me down to the floor to sit by her knees. She'd say, "You're too big to sit in my lap; my knees hurt." She'd listen to me tell her about my day. One of our ongoing conversations was about this boy that I really liked who would tease me and play with me, but I knew he didn't like me the way I liked him. She would say, "Baby, you can't make anybody love you.

You just have to be yourself, and you'll find the right one." I thought she was so wise. As I watched the EMS team take her out, I just thought my heart would literally break into pieces.

# PART 3.
# ADULT WORLD
# & HIGHER
# EDUCATION

# 10

# On Our Own

*"I began to understand that suffering and dis-
appointments and melancholy are there not
to vex us or cheapen us or deprive us of our
dignity but to mature and transfigure us."*
— Hermann Hesse, Peter Camenzind

**I used to** hear my affluent white peers talking about
taking the SATs and prepping for college. I may have
even taken the SAT because of an expectation based
on the classes I were assigned. I didn't really know
what they were talking about and didn't care. I had
no thoughts of going to college. There was no talk in
my home or community, and definitely no money for
it. The norm in the community was that people graduated from high school, if they didn't simply drop
out. They either continued to work in the tobacco

fields, repeating the cycle of becoming sharecroppers, or they branched into the industrial world and went to Dan River Mills to work in the cotton factory. A lucky few were hired on at Goodyear Tire and Rubber Co. I didn't know anything about scholarships or loans. School counselors had no conversations about continuing my education, though I had good grades. The conversation at my home, and most other homes in the sharecroppers' community, was get a job or work in the fields. Doing nothing was not an option.

After graduation, I thought I'd finish the summer helping my Dad with the tobacco crop and then get a job at "The Mill" in the fall. At best, my dream job was to become a secretary some place, someday. I had taken Typing 1-4 and Shorthand 1-4 in high school. I visualized myself sitting behind a desk with my legs crossed, taking dictations from my boss, quickly typing notes, and proudly presenting the finished product back to him. Of course, being a secretary didn't happen. I never thought of a lady leading!.

In the fall after graduation, I got a job at Dan River Mills in Danville in the weave room. Oh, how I hated that job! I cried every day. My job was to keep the looms running. My looms would sometimes seemed to be in concert and directed by a conductor to all stop at once; dust and mist floated all around me like snowflakes in the middle of a mild rain, and the supervisor squawked past my work area constantly, rolling his eyes and screaming at me to "Get those looms going." My brother, Willie "Ed", worked in the same department and would try to help me whenever he could. I used to think, "There has to be a better way to make a living than this." I looked around and saw so many older ladies, bodies bent over like a straining bow, doubled from years of hard, physical labor, trying to get looms started.

My girlfriend, Rosa Poole, unexpectedly came to my rescue. One day in the spring, following my high school graduation, she called and told me about a teacher assistant job that was available at Dan River Elementary School in Pittsylvania County, VA, where she worked. I didn't know what that job was, but it sounded exciting. She explained that it was helping the teacher help the kids with their work, putting up bulletin boards, grading papers and things like that.

She advised me how to dress for the interview. "Go out and find a dark skirt and white blouse," she said. "Do not come with your mid-drift showing," she said strongly. She knew it was my usual mode of dress. After all, I had a cute little body and loved showing it off whenever possible. I was hired for the job and introduced to the world of public education as a teacher assistant for Title I math. I loved the work, and I learned from a teacher, Joan Moore, who made learning fun and engaging for students. She included me in planning and presenting the lessons. I could not believe that I was getting paid to do work that I so enjoyed.

While working at Dan River Elementary, I married my high school sweetheart. We were so young. Two years later, we had a beautiful son, Draper. We separated when I turned 23. I realized that my marriage was not going to work. We still lived in the sharecropper's shack in poverty with my father, my sister, Emma and her two children. On cold nights, as I rocked my beautiful son to sleep, wrapped in a quilt to keep warm by the wood stove that only had a few embers of warmth, I used to rack my brain thinking about how I might get us out of poverty.

Emma and I shared single motherhood simultaneously. Emma had two children, Myesha and Marco; I had Draper. Our children were close in age. Draper and Marco were five months apart, and Myesha two years older. One day when our boys were nearly two and Myesha nearing four, Emma and I decided to pool our resources and rent a place together to raise our children. We wanted to get from under our Daddy's roof and, hopefully, provide better for them.

We inquired about a run-down, vacant shack in the neighborhood. Though the owner acknowledged that the place wasn't "fit to live in," he agreed to rent it to us for $40 a month. Though in poor condition, it was no worse than our current dwelling. The tiny little house had two very small bedrooms, no bathroom, no running water, and a kitchen that was a closed in back porch. It had thin glassed windows with no insulation. There was a small, tin, wood-burning stove in the living room that provided the heat for the entire house. Sometimes, the pipe reaching through the ceiling would tumble down as the fire burned. Emma spent numerous hours putting the pieces back together again with a wire clothe hanger. Emma, Myesha and Marco shared the larger bedroom that was large enough to accommodate a full-sized bed, a twin bed, and dresser with barely walking space between. They had what we considered a large closet, maybe 4' x 7', that held their belongings. Draper and I shared the smaller room with a full-size bed and a baby crib. A bedside table with drawers and a small closet about 2'x3" held our things; boxes under the bed served as storage for the remainder of our belongings.

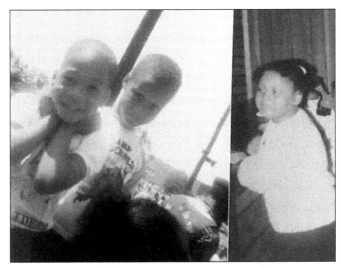
Our children - Draper, Marco, & Myesha

Our grandmother lived near us, about 500 yards away; our grandfather had passed several years earlier. Each day, to get our supply of water for drinking and cooking, we would fill five-gallon buckets with water from her outside spigot and track it back home. With Emma on one side and I on the other, we'd insert a sturdy tree limb or stick under the bucket handle and transport the liquid home. Occasionally, we'd transport several 5-gallon buckets in the trunk of the car.

Always the fixer, Emma basically took care of the household. She was self-taught on how to fix small things that broke like door and dresser knobs, the chimney pipe, light fixtures, etc. Emma could do anything with a pair of pliers and a wire clothes hanger!

Emma was gifted in repurposing materials to enhance our lifestyle!!!! Her talents went beyond being handy with a pair of pliers. To decorate the run-down place, she made curtains and hung white paneling. We purchased a used brown, red, black and white plaid living room suite from Schewel Furniture Store. We made a cozy place for our children and us, at least cozy in the spring.

Like most of our neighbors, summers found us battling the heat. One electric fan was a norm for all the folks we knew. The winter months, however, created another story all together. To fuel the one wood stove, we had a routine. On the many cold days that greeted us with either snow or below freezing temperatures, Emma would start the day early. She'd dress in several layers of clothing. She'd double and triple wrap in sweaters, socks, hats, and coats. She'd wrap her shoes in plastic, loaf bread bags to ward off the wet, and then pull on her old work gloves that she constantly mended. Clad in her work wear, Emma headed out to the surrounding woods with her axe. She'd spend a couple of hours chopping tree limbs and dragging them to the house. From time to time, she'd come in the house to warm her hands, sometimes with near frozen tears on her face, and head back out. Emma repeated the process until she felt she had enough fuel to last us through the night. After warming, she'd spend more hours outside axe-chopping the wood into sections to fit our tiny tin stove and stacking the logs on the front porch. We didn't have a back porch. Sometimes, I'd pitch in to drag the logs to the house and help with the chopping and stacking. My role, mostly, was watching the children, as I lacked the physical strength and skills of wood cutting that Emma possessed. Daddy, occasionally, would bring us a load of wood, but it only lasted a few days, and Emma and I would be right back to the axe-swinging task.

I sometimes wondered how we would have survived without Emma's skills. I agonizingly recall one incident after Emma began working at the nursing home as a certified nursing assistant. A snowstorm came along in the evening, and due to the severity of the storm, Emma was unable to make it home from work, and thus, unable to get limbs from the woods for firewood. I was an elementary school teacher at that time, and school was closed due to inclement weather. I was home with the children. As evening closed in and the last flames from the dying logs had nearly extinguished, I remember putting all three children in bed with me. We cuddled, said our prayers, and I assured them that everything would be fine. I silently cried all night long, wondering what we would do the next day without heat. In the middle of the night, I decided that we would walk to my grandmother's house for a while and then decide what to do after that. I cried some more and prayed for God to help us. The next morning, I woke to a thump, thump, thump on the front porch. Opening the door, I discovered Wesley Williams, a neighbor, throwing large logs onto the front porch. He said that he rode passed our house and saw that we had no wood and just had to stop and help. I cried even harder, but this time with joy and thanked God. I continue to give Him thanks, even to this day.

Emma was the caretaker, no doubt. She took care of the house while I worked outside the home. She could make a meal of anything. Monthly, we'd use our food stamps to purchase white potatoes, beans, rice, flour and corn meal, hearty foods so that we could eat throughout the month. We'd also go to Old Dutch Supermarket and buy meats - a chicken or small piece of beef – on sale because they were close to the expiration date, and Emma would make several delicious meals. Even though unhealthy (lots of starches), our stomachs were full the first three weeks of the month, thanks to those food stamps. The last week was tough. Emma scrounged to find enough food for us to eat, and we'd anxiously wait for the next month's lauded stamps.

Though challenging times, there were great

moments in our little house. For instance, we loved making a special event of watching holiday animated programs like "Rudolph the Red Nosed Reindeer" and "Charlie Brown's Christmas." We'd make it a family popcorn picnic on the floor with the kids. We enjoyed prepping the children for church programs, hearing them sing in the choir, and helping them memorize lines for church plays. Emma and I made a home out of nothing and filled it with joy in the midst of the challenges.

# 11

# On to Higher Education

*"Success is no accident. It is hard work, per-severance, learning, studying, sacrifice and most of all, love of what you are doing or learning to do."*

- Pele

**In the spring** (1978) of my fourth year as a teacher assistant, federal funding cuts meant that many teacher assistant positions were being eliminated. Conversations about reassignments and downsizing dominated discussion in the school. In a conversation with my friend Rosa, who was responsible for my getting the job, she told me that she was going to Averett College in Danville. I asked if I could go too. She replied, "Sure." Rosa proceeded to explain that she did not know what she was doing, did not have any money, but I could go with her to the school to learn what we could. So, we trekked to Averett and were introduced to the Financial Aid Officer, Dr. Faulk, if my memory is correct. He asked us many questions about our goals and financial status. We had no clue of the processes or protocols for entering college, but we were answering and asking questions. I suspect I was talking fast, as usual, because I remember Dr. Faulk saying, "Anyone who wants to go to school as badly as you do will do well. I'm going to help you," and he did.

One requirement for admittance to Averett was evidence of income for the past few years. For some reason, I needed evidence of my father's income because of the time frame between living with him and moving in with Emma. When I explained to Dr. Faulk that Daddy was a sharecropper and did not get standard pay stubs or W2s, he suggested that a written statement from the landowner of the total earnings for the year in question would suffice. That sounded simple enough to me.

I went to the landowner with my request. Beforehand, as suggested by Dr. Faulk, I'd written a simple statement on notepaper, something similar to, "I verify that income earned by Johnnie Richardson for [year stated] was _____." I'd already written in the date. All that was needed was for the landowner to fill in the amount and sign on the dotted line; I expected this to be an easy task. When I presented the paper to the landowner, he cursed me and told me that he would not give me any information, nor would he sign the form. I was shocked. With a few additional profanities, he commanded that I get off his land immediately. By this time, I was feeling desperate, thinking that I would not have a chance to get into Averett without this statement. Not sure where the thought came from, I told him that I would be back with my attorney to get the statement. He jerked the paper out of my hands, wrote down a dollar amount, signed the form and tossed it at my feet. He, again, cursed me profusely, including the use of the "N" word. He demanded that I leave his property and never return, or he'd have me arrested. Confused at his reaction, I left, but I was happy that I had the document I needed to proceed with entering Averett. I realized later that the landowner's anger was likely because he knew he had not given my father fair wages and was hesitant to document such.

When I told my family that I was going to college, they were pleased, but skeptical. Like me, they did not really know what that meant. After all, I was a single parent of one child, renting a house ($40 monthly) with my sister and her two children, and would have no income. My oldest brother, Johnny Jr., angrily ignited, "What's wrong with you? You must be crazy because you know you gotta work and have a child to take care of. How are you gonna feed him? Who's gonna pay your bills?"

It wasn't that Johnnie did not want to see me prosper; he was really concerned for my welfare. He had witnessed earlier struggles and hardships, and like me, did not really comprehend how this would work. I, too, wondered, "Am I crazy? How am I going to make it? How will I feed my baby?" I remember sharing these thoughts with my oldest sister, Bessie Mae, who lived in San Diego. She said, "Annie, I bet you can get on welfare" and explained the process. Getting into the social system had never occurred to me. I had always worked and had no idea what it entailed. I went to the office in Halifax, Virginia, to inquire. The social service workers were surprised and pleasantly helpful. I was told that they had not worked with anyone trying to continue their education, so they constantly called the cooperate office in Richmond, Virginia, for guidance. These calls continued throughout the three years I renewed for services.

Finally, I was an official student at Averett College. For economic reasons, Rosa and I carpooled the nearly 30 miles in our old vehicles with Rosa driving one week, and I would drive the next. On her week, she'd drive her jalopy with the rusting roof and a stick propping up the broken driver's seat. I'd follow the next week, driving my sky blue, 1972 heatless Pontiac Le Mans Coupe, with the brown bumper (accident replacement by previous owner) with no heat. We'd cover our legs with an old blanket for warmth and kept on our coats. It was most challenging, especially in the cold winter months when it snowed. We'd breathe a prayer of thanksgiving whenever we arrived at Averett and returned home safely.

Rosa and I both started Averett majoring in education. She later decided to change her major to business administration. I found the professors to be caring and personable, and I discovered that I truly loved the learning process. I was being exposed to a different kind of thinking, different genres of literate, diversity in a student population, people who had conversations and experiences beyond farming and rural living. I was totally fascinated.

At the time of my attendance, Averett offered its traditional semesters of coursework and additional learning opportunities that we called "mini-mesters", courses between the traditional semesters. By taking courses during the "mini-mesters," Rosa and I were able to complete the four-year program in three years. I graduated Cum Laude with a bachelor's degree in Elementary Education, in May 1981; this was a life-changing moment.

Though he told me how crazy I was to quit my job, Johnnie, my oldest brother, was in the audience with wife Ann and children, cheering me on. My sister Emma, her two children, Myesha and Marco, and my son, Draper, were also among the well-wishers. I walked across the stage excited, and proud, earning a bachelor's degree. Praise God!!!! [This was the first of four degrees as I later earned a Master of Education and Education Specialist from the University of Virginia in Charlottesville, Virginia and later an Educational Doctorate from Fayetteville State University in North Carolina.] Anxiety persisted, however, because upon earning this bachelor's degree, I still did not have a job and continued to live in poverty.

# PART 4.
# K-12 CAREER

# 12

# Good News!
# I'm a Teacher

*"What a teacher is, is more important than
what he teaches."*
- Margaret E. Sangsters

**In 1981, teaching** jobs across the country were scarce. Nowhere was the scarcity felt more than the South, and in deep Southside Virginia, it was as heavy as a wet blanket. I applied to all the local counties – Pittsylvania, Halifax, Mecklenburg, and Martinsville. I interviewed in the last three and received job offers in all of them. I preferred Halifax, of course. It was home. I was a single mom, had little to no income, and the thought of relocating was more than intimidating. I interviewed with Superintendent Udy Wood, an aging, round faced, heavy jawed, Caucasian, with peering eyes. As he intently studied me and asked questions, I could tell that he favored me with my answers and my looks, finding me acceptable. At the end of the interview, he told me that he thought I'd fit quite well at C.H. Friend Elementary in South Boston City Schools. He told me to call Doyle Bryson, principal, and gave me the telephone number and address to the school. I left excited and headed downtown.

Halifax County Schools and South Boston City Schools were considered two separate systems at the time. Many considered the city schools to be more prestigious. One reason for this perception was the old stigma that "city" was good and ahead of the times and "country" was less informed. Another reason may have been that many of the business leaders, doctors, lawyers, teachers, etc. lived in the city, and this is where many of their children attended. Rural Halifax was still dominated by tobacco farmers, sharecroppers and a few factory workers.

Doyle Bryson welcomed me as a fourth-grade teacher, and I was so excited to be assigned to Room 48 to begin my teaching career. I remember sitting in a pre-school faculty meeting in the cafeteria with fellow teachers as Mr. Bryson issued our student lists written on index cards. Two veteran teachers straddling me with one sitting to my left and the other to my right, peeked at my cards and started giggling. When I asked why the giggles, they said, "You've got skid row." I was so ignorant at that time and smiled back at them without a clue as to what they meant by such a comment. I later learned that by skid row, they had written my students off as having no future because most of them had been retained at least twice, some more. Those teachers had already decided that these children were prison bound. The kids were basically poor, black and male, except for one little black girl in the mix. In the educational field, it was called "grouping," and this was my introduction.

I discovered, however, that the children were wonderful and wanted to learn. They wanted and needed attention. Hands-on learning was their mode of learning, and they responded beautifully to encouragement, respect and care. Having lived in the world of poverty, I understood their needs and made concerted efforts to meet them. As a result, we had an extraordinary year! As a matter of fact, we had such a successful year that the following year and years to come were filled with requests from affluent parents wanting their children in my class, including the principal and peer teachers.

I loved teaching, but at home, we were still struggling with poverty in our cold, waterless shack. On days when school was closed early due to inclement weather, I probably regretted it much more than the students because I knew that it would be a long, cold day and an even longer night at my home.

# 13

# Administration
# and Supervision

*"Before you are a leader, success is all about growing yourself. When you become a leader, success is all about growing others."*
- Jack Welch

**After teaching a** few years, I was hired as Title I (now Chapter 1) Supervisor in Halifax County, Virginia. Though thrilled at the promotion, I cried as I packed my few belongings in cardboard boxes and carried them from my classroom to my car. I loved teaching, but as a single mother still living in poverty, I welcomed the $10k raise, and I looked forward to the opportunity to build capacity in teacher leaders. As Title I Supervisor, my charge was to work with the Federal

Programs Director, ensuring guidelines were followed as we focused on meeting the needs of educationally deprived children from low-income families.

Halifax County and South Boston schools had merged as one school district, and I'd earned my master's degree in Curriculum & Instruction from the University of Virginia and began work that would later lead to an Education Specialist degree. It was during this time that I met my future spouse, Ray, a Staff Sergeant in the United States Army, stationed in Fort Eustis, VA. This encounter opened new doors to a new life and many new learning and leadership opportunities.

Some would describe our meeting as accidental, and others might describe it as divine. We'd prefer divine. My friend, Rosa again, was part of a professional group called Dan Valley American Business Women's Association that sponsored an overnight excursion and harbor dinner cruise to Newport News. The location was about four hours east of Halifax, and I'd never been on a "cruise" before. The bus load of about 50 women arrived at the dock, but we were told that we had to wait for the disc jockey (DJ) to arrive and set up before boarding. Rosa and I were standing next to each other as the DJ arrived in a cream-colored van with brown doors. Sitting on the passenger side was this gorgeous, muscular hunk wearing a lemon-yellow shirt. I looked at him pointedly and said to Rosa,

"That one's mine." She laughed and said, "Girl, you are crazy." I said, "Just watch; he's mine."

Three years later, in June 1990, Ray and I were married with our children as part of the ceremony. Draper walked me down the aisle of Mt. Grove Missionary Baptist Church, South Boston, VA, and Tavon (my new son through Ray) served as Ray's Junior Best Man. A week later, in the middle of many tears, Ray, Draper, Tavon and I packed our belongings in a U-Haul and headed further south to Savannah, GA, where Ray was now stationed at Hunter Army Airfield.

L to R: Draper, Annie, Ray, Tavon

## Principal Leadership

I applied for a teaching position with Savannah-Chatham Public Schools. When I arrived for the interview, the Director of Personnel said, "With your credentials, you should be applying for an administrator's position. We are opening a new elementary school. Do you mind if I submit your name for an interview?" She then called the principal of East Broad Street Elementary and arranged the interview. I was hired on the spot for the assistant principal role of this magnet academy, one of the first new schools built in nearly 30 years, I was told. With the white male principal, we selected curriculum, furniture, materials and supplies, and all things that come with building and staffing a new facility. The leader, a divorced male, maintained control of hiring the bulk of the staff, mostly young, beautiful white girls right out of college.

Near the end of the staffing process when most of the teaching crew had been identified, the principal mentioned to me that we needed to add some diversity to the staff. I am not sure if this was his idea or if it had been directed to him from central office because most of the students identified to attend this school were African American. This high tech (for 1990) magnet school had been built in downtown Savannah with the purpose of drawing more and more white students to the inner city. The principal said to me, "Annie, I want you to hire some black teachers. If they are breathing, hire them." I was stunned that breathing was the only criteria he expected of black teachers.

This new assignment was my first official administrative role at a school site, and it was most challenging. Structure, guidance, and school operational procedures were sorely lacking for this new facility. No operational manual or protocols were provided. Though there were many strong teachers, weak teaching and low levels of learning dominated this spanking new edifice. Many teachers, mostly Caucasian, young, single and recent college graduates, struggled with pedagogy and classroom management. They lacked the skills for engaging a predominantly black student population. At the end of the first semester, the original, laissez-faire principal leader was replaced after impregnating a kindergarten teacher. Replacing him was the total opposite personality and leadership style, an autocratic female leader who stated often and loudly, "No one makes any decisions around this place until they go through me." The culture certainly changed. Though one of fear, expectations were clear, and there was a significant improvement in the climate. My thinking as a school leader was being shaped with ideas of what to do and what not to do from both chiefs.

About two and a half years later, another elementary school was being built in a fast-growing community known as Georgetown, a community supposedly established by white flight. I was told, a group of people left the inner city to create a homo-geneous group. Much overt and convert surprise was expressed when I was hired to lead this new commu-nity school, named Georgetown Elementary School. Immediately after being named the principal, I was invited to a community meeting at the Club House and found myself to be one of a few, if not the only, African American in a packed house of Caucasian parents and community members who peered and studied me suspiciously. They politely questioned me, and it ended with "We'll be keeping up with you", their way of saying, "We'll be watching you." Over the course of time, many of these same parents be-came my best allies as we en- joyed milestone after milestone of success.

At Georgetown, as with East Broad Magnet Academy, I had the pleasure of facilitating the staff-ing, curriculum, furnishing, etc. The major difference, however, was the learning that I carried from the ex-perience at East Broad Magnet (good and bad) and the guidance of a strong coach, Assistant Superintendent Beverly Oliver. With her guidance, I was able to staff the school with what I often described as the best staff in the district, state and even the world. Beverly would often say, "Annie, your staff is no better than anyone else's. You make them believe that they are the best, and thus, they perform that way." There are so many wonderful experiences from Georgetown Elementary that stories could fill its own book [maybe next edition].

Six or so years later, I was hired to serve as leader in opening the new middle school, Southwest Middle School. People said, "Girl, you have to be touched to work with middle school kids; they're crazy." I guess I must have been touched because I absolutely loved it. The tremendous experience of staffing, curriculum, team-building, furnishing, supplies, etc. was deja vu. Yes, again, I had the BEST staff on the East coast and often bragged ~~~~~ rned so many lessons.

East Broad Street Elementary

Georgetown Elementary

Southwest Middle School

## 6 Leadership Lessons Learned as a Principal

1. Have a vision and share it. I believed that all children could soar to high heights in learning. Thus, at Georgetown Elementary, we stole R. Kelly's song, "I believe I can fly." [**NOTE:** R. Kelly is facing massive legal allegations at the time of this writing, and his mention here is not to be interpreted as an endorsement of his accused behavior. The lyrics of his song were most appropriate for us in the 90s.] We talked about what that meant to us about believing in self and achieving higher academic standards. As I walked down the hallways greeting students, parents, staff, it was a norm to break out in song, "I believe I can fly", and we began to believe that. At Southwest, we touted, "If you want to hang with the Eagles, you've gotta learn how to fly." We believed that we had a unique culture of high performance, and students and staff used this motto to encourage and redirect positive behavior. It seemed to work!!!

2. Build relationships. I instinctively knew that getting to know internal people (students, teachers, custodians, cafeteria workers and all) and external folks (parents and community) was crucial. Maybe I'd been told this in

some of my college courses, but it became real as I operated as leader. I needed buy-in to promote the vision for the school, and those strong relationships were key. I talked to people, ask questions about their lives – personal and professional -- shared information about self, invited all into the school, asked their opinions and used that feedback for changes. This helped the school become their school, our school.

3. Be visible. I walked to every classroom practically every day saying "Good morning boys and girls," (elementary school) and "Good morning young people" (middle school).

Students responded in unison in call back fashion saying, "Good morning Ms. Wimbish." This became a ritual, and students and staff expected to see me; if I missed a day, the next day, several people (students and staff) would greet me with, "we missed you yesterday." This visit gave me time to get to know the people and to also monitor what was happening in classrooms. I attended little league games, church worship services, and student performances outside of school. I shopped at Walmart and local places where the people shopped (until I needed a break – anonymity. Ha! Ha!).

4. Show passion. If you're excited about what's happening, others will be too. I was demanding and commanding. However, I laughed, shouted and cried with the rest when encountering successes and failures.

5. Always carry self with dignity and demonstrate moral values. I was aware that people watched everything I said or did, even when I was unaware. For example, I had a community person say, "I know you like [named product] because my sister works at Walmart, and she said she sees you purchase it." I was reminded to be even more careful of what I purchased, what I said, and where I spent my time. People notice EVERYTHING.

6. Have fun, even while holding people to high expectations. I'd laugh and joke with teachers and students and offered myself as an incentive for increased learning. For example, I sat in a tub of Jell-O and read "The Principal from the Black Lagoon." I was dumped in the water tank. I dressed up as book characters. I lip sang as Diana Ross with male teachers as my Supremes. Yes, we had fun. But when time for teaching and learning, I expected teachers to be in classrooms with students engaged on required standards. When not on task,

specific feedback was swiftly given and generally the situation was corrected immediately. I had faculty and staff say to me that I expected too much from them as employees at other schools did not have to work as hard. My response was always the same. "My charge is to make sure that our kids have the best because they deserve it; that's what I'd want for my personal children. If you want to work 'less hard,' I'll help you get to one of these other places that do not require much."- None of those complainers ever voluntarily left.

## Assistant Superintendent

In 2000, my previous superintendent recruited me to Moore County, NC, as Assistant Superintendent. I loved Savannah, and hesitated leaving. However, my father had been diagnosed with cancer in Virginia, and I wanted to be closer to home. Moore County was only about 3.5 hours from my hometown verses the seven hours from Savannah. I applied, was hired, and was basically an area superintendent.

There were 22 schools in the district at that time, divided as North Moore and South Moore. I was responsible for overseeing the Southern Schools, and Dr. Donna Peters was responsible for the Northern Schools; Donna and I were the first female assistant superintendents (one black and one white) in Moore County, and we began to crack the glass ceiling. There had been only one other African American leader, a black male, at central office prior to me, and from the stares and questionable looks, it was clear that people were skeptical of what to expect. Donna and I quickly became friends and worked well to support principals, and schools, taking pride as they soared to high academic levels. Donna was more the right brain thinker, seeing the big picture and coming up with the creative and innovative ideas. I was more of a left-brain thinker, focusing on implementation, details and follow-up. We made a dynamic team despite the superintendent's quest for us to be competitors.

Of the 22 principals in Moore County, two were Black. I remember how George, a veteran white male high school principal, quickly pulled me to the side and said to me, "Annie, I know you want to do a good job and seem to be an independent lady, but don't go riding these back roads alone at night." When asked why, he said, "Remember, you are still in the South." I was so surprised and somewhat frightened, as I'd never directly experienced racism.

I found Moore County to be an interesting place to live and work, though there were very few African American leaders. From my view, there were "haves and have nots" and very few in-betweens. I was welcomed into circles and invited to serve on many civic boards of trustees, like Sandhills Boys and Girls Club, SMART START/Moore County Partners for Children and Families, and First Health of the Carolinas Community. I also enjoyed being a member of Carthage Rotary, one of few minorities. Numerous times I reflected on how a sharecropper's daughter could serve as a leader in a community like Moore County. My grandmother would have been shocked and tickled to death as I recalled her excitedly telling the story with pride (countless times, I may add) of how important she felt when the "white man" (farm owner) let her ride in the front seat of his truck with him and his wife. Whew!

After working in Moore for a couple of years, another veteran principal said, "Annie, when you were hired, we principals were hell bent and determined not to like you and made a pack to help you fail. We believe any of us could have been hired to be Assistant Superintendent. However, after getting to know you, and we saw how you cared for us and treated us with respect, we came to love you and only wanted you to be successful." Wow, I was again shocked, surprised and humbled.

# 14

# Superintendent of Schools

*"The challenge of leadership is to be strong,
but not rude; be kind, but not weak; be bold,
but not a bully; be thoughtful, but not lazy;
be humble, but not timid; be proud, but not
arrogant; have humor, but without folly."*

- Jim Rohn

Hattiesburg Public School District Administrative Offices, 2005

**After serving as** Assistant Superintendent in Moore County for five years, I was ready for my next challenge. I had this history of serving three to five years in a role before getting the transitional "itch", I called it. I'd earned my doctorate from Fayetteville State University in Fayetteville, N.C., December 2004 and was ready to exploit my new knowledge. I'd applied for a superintendent's position at a couple of places in North Carolina and one in Virginia, always thinking of being closer to home. One day I received a call from a Superintendent Search Agency to inquire of my interest in applying in Hattiesburg, Mississippi. I'd never heard of Hattiesburg and had only been to southern Mississippi once while on vacation at Beau Rivage Golf and Resort in Gulfport, MS. My perception of Mississippi was very negative, and that perception was based on what I'd seen on television and heard from others – high poverty, high teenage pregnancy, low educational attainment, etc. I perceived an image of immense poverty---women barefoot and pregnant with no teeth, living on dirt roads, and still using outhouses. Still, I submitted the resume.

I was surprised when I got the call for an interview. Even as I was flying to Gulfport, MS, for the interview, I was on the plane thinking, "Girl, why are you wasting your time like this? You know that you don't want to go to Mississippi." I got off the plane, rented a car, and drove 49 North to Hattiesburg. I remember this strange feeling that came over me, like déjà vu. It was as if I'd been there before; something felt so familiar. A calm, happy feeling enveloped me, like going home. When I turned onto Mamie Street, I smiled, and really didn't know why.

Because I arrived early for the interview, I rode around town, taking in the sites: homes, restaurants, University of Southern Mississippi, people movements, and the like. I stopped at the local McDonald's on Hardy Street to grab a bite. I'd learned long ago that if you want to know the truth about a place, talk to the people who live there. I made it a point to strike up conversations with people about how long they'd lived in Hattiesburg; what they liked and disliked; what the school system was like, to get a feel from the people. Hearing their responses, I realized that my image of backward folk, all in rural poverty, at least in Hattiesburg, was so wrong. Yes, there was poverty a plenty, but there was so much more. In those short conversations, I learned that the people were informed with high standards and high expectations. I left McDonald's with the thought that though there were challenges, Hattiesburg Public Schools had great potential. Living in Hattiesburg became an inviting, appealing prospect.

I arrived at 301 Mamie Street, location of the

Administrative Building for Hattiesburg Public Schools. Greeted by serene, professional, quiet-spoken, Ms. Bonnie Hill, the superintendent's administrative assistant, she ushered me into the empty superintendent's office to wait for my appointed time. The complex was an old building, with high ceilings and spacious. The superintendent's office was like so, with high windows that invited natural light. Adjourning was a large conference room where the Board of Trustees had gathered behind closed doors prior to the interview. Again, I felt so comfortable and relaxed as I waited. I felt totally at home.

Four of the five members of the Board of Trustees attended the interview; the fifth joined us from out of the country via telephone. I connected well with the Board members and they to me. I flew back to Moore County, and the following day, I was offered the job; I still reel at the speed of the decision and my surprise.

My husband, Ray, was in Iraq, working on a contract for Haliburton. He had no idea that I had applied for, let alone interviewed for, the job. When he made his routine call, I told him that I was going to Hattiesburg. His reaction was, "Going where? Hattiesburg? Why in the hell do you want to go to Hattiesburg?". His reaction was based on a brief stopover in Hattiesburg in the late 80's at Camp Shelby Military Base. From his short stay, his perception of

Hattiesburg was that it was rural, isolated, segregated, and very little to offer in recreation and entertainment. After I explained my feelings of "being home" there and how things appeared totally different from his 80's experience, he responded, "OK baby, if that's what you want, you know that I am there for you." We were ready for the move.

Ray flew home from Iraq for a few days to supervise the moving and the movers, as they packed us up in Moore County, North Carolina, to head for Mississippi. By the way, God sent us a buyer for our home before we even put it on the market! We loaded the two cars (Ray in the 2002 Trooper and I, in my doctorate graduation gift from him, a 2001 Mercedes E320). I was basking in my blessings – new degree, new car, new job!!!

My first day on the job as superintendent was scheduled for July 1, 2005. There was a community function on the evening of June 30th (my 50th birthday), and I was invited to give brief remarks as an introduction to the community. Ray and I arrived in Hattiesburg in our two-car caravan around 4:30 pm on June 30, after a long drive from Moore County, NC. The Board of Trustees had arranged temporary housing – a small, furnished, two-bedroom apartment -- as part of my contract to allow time for a permanent home search. Because of the narrow time frame of our arrival and the program starting time, we parked, grabbed a suitcase with essentials, ran into the apartment, changed hastily for the program, and rushed off to Trinity Episcopal Church, where the function took place.

I had my first inkling of what it would be like to be Superintendent of Hattiesburg Public Schools when I arrived at the church. All eyes were on me and each move scrutinized as though through a microscope. It was my new existence. The press was there, cameras were flashing, people were whispering, "There she is; that's the new superintendent." My knees shook, as the enormity of the role began to sink in. I found the people curious, yet welcoming. I was the first female and only the second African American superintendent, making the highest salary of any superintendent in Mississippi at that time. History was being made. I was awed, honored, scared, and confident. I knew that feelings of anxiety had to be held at bay. That was the first of many receptions and speaking invitations to follow. Most were positive and encouraging.

Ray only had a few days before he returned to Iraq. While he spent the days with a realtor, searching for our new home, I spent the days making the rounds, meeting faculty, staff and community members. In the evenings, he and I compared notes, and he'd be off again. He narrowed the search to four houses. We chose one. Leaving me with his Power of Attorney, after a week, Ray flew back to Iraq. I continued to live in the apartment, waiting for the home closing procedure. The closing happened on August 26, and I made arrangements for our furniture to be delivered from storage in Moore County.

The first few weeks, I met the staff and community, all curious as expected of the new superintendent. One black teacher told me that she had planned to retire. After hearing that I was hired, she was encouraged and decided to stay on for at least one more year. I was flattered but certainly felt the pressure of high expectations. I would hear whispers and get cautious and excited looks wherever I went. I met with staff members in large and small groups for introductions and to build my knowledge of them. They sold themselves and their levels of importance in a multitude of ways. One came with a compact disc of her department's profile; one put together a profile of all the department heads and member roles. One even came with a new organizational structure with several new assistant superintendent positions that included himself. As one director expounded on her level of importance in supervising principals, she asked, "How do you 'make' them [principals] do what you tell them to do?" I knew that building collaborative leadership skills had to be added to the top of the list of focus in

Hattiesburg Public Schools, for I believe that effective leaders don't "make" people do things; they lead them instead.

The press fed the curiosity of the citizens with a daily article (it seemed) of my movements. Sadly, one of the first articles showed a beautiful colored photo of me speaking with a group of primary, African American students. Its content focused more on my appearance and less on my leadership skills, as the article described my "pretty ears." I was very disappointed and became even more determined to make a difference. I held onto the belief that many of the folk were sincerely interested in helping children. I saw guidance on the direction for the district was the greatest need for the success.

## Here Comes Katrina!!!

I'd been in Hattiesburg for a little under two months when the weather predictions rallied warnings of a pending level four hurricane hitting our area, but I paid little attention with all the excitement of relocating and starting the new job – such adjustments. Too, I'd never experienced a hurricane and had no idea of what that might mean. I did, however, pick up a 24-pack of bottled water and a couple of extra canned goods from the supermarket. I also filled both cars with gasoline on Sunday, August 28, after attending

11:00 am worship service at Ebenezer Baptist Church.

On Monday, August 29, 2005, Hurricane Katrina hit with all of its Level 4 vengeance. It was surreal to me. I'd never been closer to a hurricane than viewing it on television, and I'd never seen anything like it – trees literally flying by the windows. Crazily, I found myself drawn to the balcony with some of the elderly residents of the apartment complex where I lived. I've often heard that God takes care of babies and fools. Looking back, it is clear that He surely took care of foolish me and my elderly companions.

At the end of Katrina's lashing, the City of Hattiesburg was devastated. No electricity, trees ripped through houses in every direction, blocking side streets, main streets and highways. Businesses were crushed; the city was shut down. Downed powerlines were strewn like spider webs. So much destruction! The following day, again in my foolishness, I jumped in the Trooper and drove out into the debris, trying to reach the administration office, a goal I failed. I swerved between downed trees and drove over fallen power lines. Some of them were likely live wires, but I gave it no thought. I was in a daze, amazed, in wonder at the devastation. Some people were standing outside of homes, looking on in dismay. "Oh, what to do?" their body language shouted.

I felt totally lost as I had been in Hattiesburg for only a couple of months. My knowledge of available resources was nil. I had no phone, very little food, little knowledge of the school district, no personal connections with anyone. My husband was in Iraq, and my family was back home in Virginia. I was familiar with only one route to the office and fallen trees blocked that path. With no phone service, contacting my mentor or asking anyone for help was impossible. Here I was in a new role, a new state, a new city with new rules in a new situation. I'd read Michael Watkins's *The First 90 Days*, but there was no chapter on how to deal with natural disasters like a Level 4 hurricane.

I'd met local superintendents and leaders and knew some names and titles, but this was beyond just knowing names. This was beyond intellectual knowledge or educational know how. I knew that my survival skills would kick in. I prayed a lot, and like a drum, the phrase continued to rotate in my brain, "He won't bring you to it if He won't take you through it," a phrase I'd heard several times in my home church, Mt. Grove Missionary Baptist Church in South Boston, VA. The Hurricane Katrina ordeal taught me quickly that I had to rely on God, the knowledge embedded in me as a leader, and the people He had in place.

The operational norms no longer applied as we had to analyze situations on the spot and take quick action. There was no rule book. As superintendent, I had to make new and immediate decisions and had to rely heavily on a strong sense of discernment in whose guidance to hear and what to reject. Reeling in all of the moral and ethical characteristics that I knew was as mandatory as possessing a cell phone is to a 10th grader; I had to have it!

I learned that many of the highly elected officials in Hattiesburg possessed positive leadership characteristics. Sadly, however, like any other place, some did not. Some even appeared to operate illegally. I was asked to purchase materials and items with funding outside of the designated line item because of the likelihood that it would not be discovered. I was queried to embellish purchases that were not made. I was demanded to create positions for "personal friends" because of political reasons. My belief, philosophy, and theory of operation, however, were that any decision I made must be "legal, decent and in order." Without these considerations, it was useless to approach me with a request. This, quickly and sadly, caused some leaders to suggest that I'd "forgotten where I'd come from" [meaning that I'd forgotten that I was Black as I would not play negative games]. That kind of thinking, by a couple of elected officials, often put me on the defensive for doing what I believed was right for the children and community. On the positive side, there were more officials than not who appeared to want positive outcomes for all the children and supported my leadership efforts with specific feedback. And though some of the upper management at the district level had agendas that were self-serving and not in the best interest of children, the majority wanted student success! Teachers who were left homeless because of the loss of homes, slept in cars by night and were present to teach and soothe children and each other by day. Staff put on gloves and masks as they assisted with cleaning water damaged walls and floors. Teachers taught in overcrowded classrooms pack with students who only had their words, no official records, for placement. Caring, loving and sacrificial, teachers made sure traumatic, displaced individuals had a place. I recall once at the shelter, a group was trying to convince a middle school aged evacuee from New Orleans to attend the middle school. He adamantly and angrily refused. A teacher and I pulled him to the side to engage in a private conversation, and he admitted not willing to attend school because he did not have "the right clothes." The teacher put the child in her car and drove him to a location for clothes. That was the kind of care that was evident, even as we all struggled.

After 14 days of logs and debris stacked 10-12 feet high or greater on the sides of the streets, and lines of people like refugees hoping for a cold bottle of water, businesses slowly opened their doors. Because of limited to no technology, transactions had to be done manually between businesses like home improvement stores and grocery chains and their customers. For security purposes, I guess, the general rule was to allow only a handful of customers to enter for purchasing limited amounts of goods. With limited capacity, the school district also opened its doors.

As I look back at the timeliness, my move to Hattiesburg and Hurricane Katrina's arrival happened almost simultaneously. I realize that it was God's orchestration. He was setting the tone for the work ahead. This horrendous, challenging situation laid the foundation for a city to work together. It demanded that I get to know the people intimately, and it necessitated that all hands relied on each other. It was an opportunity for me to show strength as a leader and weakness as a human being.

The first year, our focus was not simply academics - reading, writing and arithmetic - but on people, on surviving, on meeting psychological and physiological needs of kids, faculty and staff, parents and the community, many of whom were homeless, including some teachers who lived in cars. Test scores were not the focus; healthy children were. People were moving into town due to deaths and flooding in New Orleans and the Gulf Coast. They came with no documents of verification and often with nothing but the clothes on their backs. We had to take people's word of child custody, grade placements, etc. For better or worse, it seemed to work. The state and federal government graciously offered various waivers for rules and regulations for compliance which allowed schools to focus on real, immediate needs of students. Outstanding caring from teachers and staff dominated.

## Stepping In and Stepping Up

The invitations to speak at numerous social, civic, and community events continued. Audiences wanted to hear the new superintendent's vision for the Hattiesburg School District. These were sometimes encouraging, with supporters hopeful for the success of the school district that was greater than 90 percent poverty and African American. At other times, it was clear that preconceived ideas existed that the school system and its children were devalued. Hattiesburg Public Schools was somewhat surrounded by more affluent school districts like Petal and Lamar counties, where many parents who could afford to, flocked to purchase homes. With these parents went much family and community support. An example of displayed community support was evident when a Caucasian male colleague superintendent from Petal attended the Hattiesburg Rotary with me, and several Rotarians and business leaders from Hattiesburg quickly approached him about working together to make Petal School District a spotlight in the state; I stood next to this superintendent in great surprise. Though I was an active member of the Hattiesburg Rotary and served with these Rotarians for a significant amount of time, I was never approached with such an offer of support for our students and district. It was so disappointing.

Another insight I found quite interesting and surprising was the gender leadership perception; again, you may recall that I was the first (and only at the time of this writing) female superintendent to serve Hattiesburg Public School District. Occasionally, when I attended some local affair with the Associate Superintendent who was male or one of the male directors, the announcer would say, "We're glad to have the superintendent of Hattiesburg with us." Many attendees would look directly at the male accompanying me, making an assumption. I continued to be surprised as my photo appeared regularly in the local news, and there were still those who thought that the superintendent must be male. Interesting, indeed!

My supporters, local and state, outnumbered the detractors, however. Most of the board members, many influential leaders at the local colleges, elected officials, and loads of parents and staff gave full support. I served on numerous boards like United Way and Area Development Partnership/Chamber of Commerce. Together, we created copious partnerships to support student development, including founding the Hattiesburg Educational Foundation designed to raise funds and provide additional opportunities for teacher and student creativity and projects.

One particular partnership that stands out with great fondness for me is Hattiesburg Housing Authority under the leadership of Executive Director, Milan Hoze. Many of our children lived in housing complexes, and I was told that historically, parents had been disenfranchised and participation discouraged. Through the partnership with Mr. Hoze, meetings with the school district and residents were regularly scheduled to take place on the grounds of the housing complex. Mr. Hoze promoted attendance, provided a light meal, and secured appealing door prizes. With a small team, I'd meet with parents and other interested persons at the complexes to provide opportunities to hear voices from these valuable community members. Initially, participants were hesitant and distrusting and conversations focused on complaints, with a negative tone. As we continued to get to know each other, trust grew, and parents opened up; issues and solutions began to surface. Community projects like these eventually lead to Hattiesburg receiving recognition at the state level for community engagement.

My state connections grew, and I was blessed to meet and developed a relationship with Dr. Hank Bounds, Mississippi Superintendent of Education, an excellent instructional leader. He asked me to serve on the Mississippi State Superintendent's Advisory Council. In this forum, I had the opportunity to give voice to some decisions made for children in Mississippi. Through this relationship with the state superintendent, I was introduced to Cisco Systems, "an American multinational technology conglomerate headquartered in San Jose, California, in the center of Silicon Valley. Cisco Systems develops, manufactures and sells networking hardware, telecommunications equipment and other high-technology services and products" (Wikipedia). Cisco Systems adopted Hattiesburg Public Schools, along with six other local districts and invested several million dollars and introduced our teachers and children to technology that they might not have, otherwise, been exposed to. Through Cisco, we were introduced to the world of design via the Schlechty Center. It was a real life-changing experience for many and brought about a major cultural transformation.

As a new superintendent, I was excited about meeting other peers across the state and joined the

Mississippi Association for State Superintendents (MASS). I remember attending my first meetings with MASS and was struck by the large number of white males who graced the platform of leadership in a state dominated by an African American population. I began to introduce myself to leadership, striking up conversations each time I attended, until I felt comfortable enough to voice my concerns about the need for more diversity in leadership. One day, I sassily marched up to the Executive Director of MASS and in a sweet, calm, professional voice drawled, "Something's wrong with this picture; y'all really need to add some color to that board." Apparently, I made an impression because in a short while, I was asked to join the Executive Board and later became President-Elect of MASS. I retired before moving into the role of President.

Creating a positive culture for learning and improving academics were two main areas of concern for Hattiesburg Public Schools. As a result of some of the listed partnership connections, commitment and willingness to grow in leadership skills from front-line leaders (principals and central office leaders) that lead to a change in culture for schools and the district, and parents who began to get more involved in the learning process, Hattiesburg Public Schools began a mighty transformation. Many of our schools improved academic ratings based on the Mississippi

Accountability Model and demonstrated higher academic achievement. One school earned the status of Level 5 – Exemplary, a first in the history of ratings for Hattiesburg Public Schools. It was a lot of hard work, but working together made the work workable!!!!

The many accomplishments of the Hattiesburg School District could be a book in itself. I was blessed as superintendent in many ways. We developed a culture that focused on valuing students, parents and community relations. What followed was academic improvement. In 2007, I was chosen as one of Mississippi's 50 Leading Business Women and Third Finalist for 2008 Mississippi Business Woman of the Year. In 2010, Mississippi Association of Office Professionals named me 2010 Administrator of the Year. From sharecropper's daughter, to teacher assistant in Virginia, to recognized superintendent in Mississippi! Who would have dreamed it? To God be the glory!!!!

I now serve as partner and executive consultant for Leadership Solutions Group, LLC. and Vice-President for Averett University Board of Trustees, a university my mom once told me that I could not attend because the college did not admit African Americans. It strengthens my belief in the motto that I often espouse when speaking with groups. "It's not where you come from, but where you're going that makes the difference."

*"With man this is impossible, but with God all things are possible" (Matthew 19:26).*

I referred to myself as the "head learner" during my superintendent's reign because I learned so much. Here are a few major take-aways:

## 7 Leadership Lessons Learned

1. Learn to follow. After Hurricane Katrina, life was fuzzy on what to do and how to do it to get Hattiesburg Public Schools up and running. I had to learn new rules, regulations and roles. I had to rely on Emergency Management staff, follow community leads, and learn new state guidelines, some of which were being written as we went along. I had to recognize that my staff had knowledge that would take me years to learn. Following is not weakness; it's wisdom. A leader loses nothing by empowering others to lead.

2. Trust your team until you learn not to. I did not know the department heads for the district – food service, maintenance, transportation, administrators, athletics, etc. I had to watch, ask questions and rely on individuals to do their jobs and monitor as I supported. In times of much distress and stress, I knew that their

core values would show, and I could use that knowledge to build a strong system.

3. Look strong, even when you are shaking. I was new to the district, the city and the state and never experienced a hurricane. Yet, people in the schools and the community came to me for advice and help in the midst of newfound homelessness, hunger, and uncertainty. As an identified leader, I was expected to know. Even if I did not know, I reached out quickly with many questions to find answers. People needed help, and in the middle of my own confusion, loneliness and fear, I knew that I had to forget self and help them.

4. Maintain a vision and focus. Even though the city was in turmoil, the children needed structure, and we needed to get back to our purpose so that the city could get back to its focal point. The front-line leaders were corralled. We put our heads and talents together, and within 14 days, we were back at teaching and learning, though a modified version.

5. Hold people accountable. Even in crisis, children are expected to learn. Standard Operational Procedures were put into place, and staff and students were held accountable

for living up to those, even as nurturance and backrubs were provided.

6. Maintain moral values. I was amazed at some city leaders who tried to persuade me to do things underhandedly, like creating positions, or hiring friends and family, and sometimes asking for support that I knew was borderline illegal like make shady deals with funding or policy violations. My answer was always that decisions I'd support had to be "legal, decent and in order." Legal meaning it must be within the law; decent meaning that it must be something that I can look at myself the next morning and be ok; and in order meaning there must be structure that allowed for a repeat performance for others, if needed.

7. Hold your own. I was a woman (African American at that) operating in a man's world of leadership, and often not expected to have answers, give feedback and input. Much of the leadership at local and state levels was male; often their behavior implied that their expectation of me was to "look good." Several times I was at the mercy of their conversations of how I "made them look good" or the value that my "prettiness" brought to the table. I did not get invited to golf games or the fishing trips

where many decisions were made. Thus, I had to invite myself to some meetings, and when given the opportunity to "join the team" (I say loosely), I had to be assertive, but nice; aggressive, but kind; and knowledgeable without overpowering. This meant many hours researching possible topics so that I could walk into a meeting with quality and depth in my conversation instead of "fluff and stuff."

Thanks to God, I was a woman on a mission, a woman on fire....

> *ROMANS 8:32* (NIV) *"He who did not spare his own Son, but gave him up for us all— how will he not also, along with him, graciously give us all things?"*

CPSIA information can be obtained
at www.ICGtesting.com
Printed in the USA
LVHW051216260420
654467LV00003B/955

9 781977 209542